Everyday

Moon

magic

About the Author

Dorothy Morrison is a third-degree Wiccan High Priestess of the Georgian Tradition, and is currently engaged in studies with RavenMyst Circle. An avid magical practitioner for nearly thirty years, she spent many years teaching the Craft to students in the United States and Australia. She also holds an honorary governorship with The Open Hearth Foundation, a Pagan community center initiative based in Washington, D.C.

To Write to the Author

If you wish to contact the author or would like more information about this book, please write to the author in care of Llewellyn Worldwide and we will forward your request. Both the author and publisher appreciate hearing from you and learning of your enjoyment of this book and how it has helped you. Llewellyn Worldwide cannot guarantee that every letter written to the author can be answered, but all will be forwarded. Please write to:

Dorothy Morrison
% Llewellyn Worldwide
2143 Wooddale Drive
Woodbury, MN 55125-2989

Please enclose a self-addressed stamped envelope for reply, or $1.00 to cover costs. If outside U.S.A., enclose international postal reply coupon.

Many of Llewellyn's authors have websites with additional information and resources. For more information, please visit our website at www.llewellyn.com.

Everyday

Moon

magic

Spells & Rituals
for Abundant Living

DOROTHY MORRISON

Llewellyn Publications
Woodbury, Minnesota

First Edition
Eighth Printing, 2013

Book design and editing by Karin Simoneau
Cover design by Kevin R. Brown
Cover imagery © Image Club Graphics and PhotoDisc

Library of Congress Cataloging-in-Publication Data
Morrison, Dorothy, 1955–
     Everyday moon magic: spells & rituals for abundant living /
Dorothy Morrison.
         p. cm.
     Includes bibliographical references and index.
     ISBN: 978-0-7387-0249-0
         1. Magic. 2. Moon—Miscellanea. I. Title.

BF1623.M66M67 2003
133.4'3—dc22   2003060308

Llewellyn Publications
A Division of Llewellyn Worldwide Ltd.
2143 Wooddale Drive
Woodbury, MN 55125-2989
www.llewellyn.com
Llewellyn is a registered trademark of Llewellyn Worldwide Ltd.
Printed in the United States of America

Also by Dorothy Morrison

Magical Needlework

Everyday Magic

In Praise of the Crone: A Celebration of Feminine Maturity

The Whimsical Tarot

Yule: A Celebration of Light & Warmth

Bud, Blossom, & Leaf:
The Magical Herb Gardener's Handbook

The Craft: A Witch's Book of Shadows

The Craft Companion

Enchantments of the Heart

Everyday Tarot Magic

Everyday Sun Magic

Dancing the Goddess Incarnate (with Kristen Madden)

To Mary Caliendo, who holds more magic in her little finger than I can ever hope to gain . . . and more strength than I can ever hope to muster!

In memory of . . . Ellen Cannon Reed—my friend, my champion, and my fellow author—who chose to fill her life with doing for our community, rather than just dreaming about it. I miss you more than you'll ever know.

Contents

Acknowledgments

No doubt, the Moon is one of the most magical forces in our universe. Still, something even more magical exists in our world—something more powerful, more beautiful, and more incredible; something so wonderful, so enchanting, and so radiant that it's capable of inducing more raw emotion than any number of Moons put together. That magical something, of course, is a creature known as the human being.

What makes it so magical? It's the very fact that each is similar while being different. And even though the similarities are many, each comes equipped with its own personality and talents, thought patterns and ideas. Standing alone, it's nothing less than remarkable. But when combining its energies with others of the same species, the magic created brings even the impossible to fruition. Such was the case with this book.

Many human beings—far too many for me to count—wove their personal magic together to bring this book into your hands, and I owe them all a great debt of gratitude. Still, there are a few who wove their magic behind the scenes to construct the loom upon which this work was created. And it's to those remarkable people that I'd like to extend a special thank you.

To my incredible husband, Mark, who constantly offers me an unfailing sense of understanding and a deeper love than I ever dreamed possible. Simply knowing you has enriched my life more than you'll ever imagine. I absolutely adore you!

To M. R. Sellars—my partner in crime, unconscious magic, the fight against bobbleheads, and the dearest friend I've ever had—who has never failed or questioned me, even when common sense should have dictated otherwise. (Bring a shovel. We're burying the body tomorrow.)

To Trish Telesco, who not only paved the way for my career and showed me that with a little patience, some hard work, and a lot of belief, dreams really can come true, but also lent ideas for the Snow Moon section of this book. I appreciate you more than you know.

To Z. What can I say except I simply don't know how I ever got along without you! And to Hardee, for sharing this remarkable woman with me.

To Dave and Chris Norris, for the star on my door, the carpet under my feet, and the Bailey's in my cup. Your love, laughter, and friendship is a treasure held close to my heart.

To Coven of the Raven for welcoming me with open arms and for making my dedication so special, and to all of RavenMyst for so graciously extending their Circle to me.

To Angel, Randal, Chell, and Duane—and all the folks at Mystic Moon Coven—whose love of the Craft never fails to inspire me, and whose love of extended family is unsurpassed.

To Karin Simoneau, my extraordinary editor, who puts up with my stubbornness, goes to bat for me, and continually makes me look good in print. I love you dearly.

To Damien Echols of the WM3, who constantly reminds me that real strength, like real magic, comes from within, and that even though life is often unfair, it never offers more than we can handle.

And finally, to you, the person who will read this book and work with the Moon's magnificent energies. Once you do, it's my hope that you'll see Her in a new light—a magical light—a light so enchanting and bewitching that you'll never view Her in the same way again.

Much love!

Dorothy

Part One

The Mystical, Magical Moon

The magical, mystical, wonderful Moon
Lights the night sky with a silvery boon
The subject of legend—the scorn of the church—
She watches the Earth from Her heavenly perch
And bathing us all with Her beauty and grace
She beckons us forward into Her embrace
For we are Her children—yes, She rules the tides
That flow through our bodies and swell and subside—
Giving courage to lovers and quickening the heart
And ruling emotions of various sorts
With whispers of magic and all it involves
Bringing personal puzzles and riddles to solve
For She is the Maiden, our Mother, the Crone
With Her joy, care, and comfort, we're never alone
And with every lunation that comes and that goes
Our love for the Moon only surges and grows

—Dorothy Morrison

1

Cultural Lunacy

The Moon is our closest neighbor, and we know a lot about Her. We know how far She lives from the Earth, the course of Her journey, and when to expect Her visits. We know about Her surface, Her terrain, and Her atmosphere. We even know the source of Her silvery iridescence. And yet, even with all these facts at hand, the Moon's power is still quite a mystery. A mystery that we shall never fully uncover or understand. A mystery that's been with us since the beginning of time and shall continue long after its end. As elusive as it is, it's this very mystery that gives the Moon such timeless appeal. It keeps us looking to Her for answers and searching out Her connections to our world. It's exactly what makes Her just as important to us today as She was to our ancestors.

Be that as it may, the Moon's significance to the world has changed somewhat with the times. It hasn't lessened, though. If anything, it's gained momentum. Think I'm kidding? Then take a look at our vocabularies. We label those whose behavior makes us crazy "lunatics," and we call the craziness that they shower upon us "lunacy."

Someone highly thought of is said to "hang the Moon." Couples in love often "moon" over each other, and a wedding vacation is known as a "honeymoon." But it doesn't stop there. The Moon also sheds light on the fields of snack food (moon pies), liquid libation (moonshine), and games of chance (shooting the Moon). Then there's that rather distasteful display of baring one's derrière—only performed by lunatics, of course—which is commonly known as "mooning."

And if craziness, love, whiskey, and childish antics weren't enough responsibility for the iridescent beauty of the night, She also figures into the entertainment business. Who, for example, could forget the trio of field mice who stole the show with their campy rendition of "Blue Moon" in the movie *Babe?* Who hasn't hummed along to the romantic strains of "Moon River?" And who hasn't felt abject terror creep into the pit of their stomachs while watching *Apollo 13?*

I could go on and on, but there isn't any need. The Moon, ancient though She is, has managed to infiltrate every fiber of our lives. She's a very real part of our modern world. And with every beam of light She casts, She becomes more firmly ingrained in our minds, our hearts, and our spirits.

But how did the Moon become so important in the first place? What roles did She play? Why was She so revered? And what first prompted our ancestors to worship Her?

THE LUNAR CLOCK

While there are many theories, one of the most valid is that the Moon—unlike the Sun—was able to change form and shape. Her crescent phase not only grew in the sky to full, round beauty, but waned again into nothingness. Even more mysteriously, She managed the process with perfect regularity. This regularity gave ancient civilizations a sound way to keep track of time,[1] and consequently the earliest calendars were based on the movement of Her cycles.

That being the case, this method of measuring time also spilled into the religious arena. The Koran, for example, not only refuses to recognize the addition of leap year days, but is firm in the fact that Islamic holidays always begin at the exact moment the Moon is seen in the sky. Of course, this means that even in the same area of the world, weather conditions—fog, rain, clouds, and so forth—may actually cause the holiday to commence at different times.

While this may seem a bit confusing, Muslims aren't the only religious sector who still use a lunar calendar to calculate celebrations. The Judaic calendar has always been based on the rising and setting of the Moon.[2] And

---

1. According to many etymologists, the word "moon" comes from a Greek word meaning "measure." The word "month" is also a derivative of "moon."

2. Though still lunar in nature, this calendar has been modernized somewhat; that is, it has been slightly modified to account for the length of the solar year.

because the early Christians calculated most of their holidays to fall in sync with Jewish festivities, we still find a connection to the Moon in many Christian celebrations with variable dates. A prime example of this is Easter, which is calculated to be "the first Sunday after the Full Moon which happens upon, or next after the twenty-first day of March."[3]

If the Moon was the original timekeeper, though, why don't we use her cycles to measure time today? How in the world did we wind up with a solar calendar?

Well, the ancient Egyptians discovered that while the Moon definitely coursed with perfect timing, Her twenty-nine day cycle didn't provide an accurate measure of the seasons. This meant that the seasonal beginnings and endings were miscalculated by several days, and this was a huge problem for the civilized world. Why? Because farmers had to know when to plant and when to harvest. Merchants had to know when they'd have crops for sale. More importantly (at least to the Egyptians) was the ability to forecast the annual flooding of the Nile River. And none of that was possible without an accurate form of seasonal measurement.

To that end, the Egyptians put their heads together and worked up a calendar based on solar cycles. The only catch was that it extended the annual calendar by eleven days, but since it put the seasons within predictability (which was the main reason for the change to

---

3. Quoted from the *English Book of Common Prayer.*

start with), it really wasn't a problem. Julius Caesar brought the calendar to Europe some two thousand years ago, and the rest, as they say, is history.

NATURAL CONNECTIONS

Another reason for the reverence to the Moon probably had to do with the direct connection of Her cycles to Nature—but most notably to the seas and oceans. Tides roll in and out with the Moon's comings and goings, and since those particular bodies of water were (at least at that point in time) considered to be the source of all life, this was very important, indeed.

The rhythms of the Moon and tide also seemed to affect all ocean-life. Shellfish and other sea creatures not only spawned and mated according to the tidal cycles, but renewed their outer shells and scales in accordance with them as well. High tide at Full Moon brought its own sort of magic. Oysters opened their shells, fish were easier to catch, and shrimp—because they have a tendency to surface and feed during that time—were plentiful.

If that weren't enough to mesmerize ancient civilizations, the Moon also had an apparent effect on other animals—animals that weren't connected with the sea at all. Game and predatory animals were much more prevalent during the Full Moon, as were birds and rodents. But that's not all. Animal behaviors changed. They became more aggressive, more physically active, and more responsive to mating rituals.

Other animal-related connections became apparent, too. Hunters discovered that game animals bled more profusely when the Moon was rising in the sky to fullness. While that bit of knowledge may seem trivial to us today, it was of incredible value to ancient livestock farmers. Why? Because it was important to conduct all stock animal slaughter swiftly. Doing so not only caused less stress on the animal, but also produced a better product, so knowing the best time to schedule this task was very handy, indeed.

Something even more important came from this information, though. By understanding when animals bled most profusely, there also came the knowledge of when they didn't. This was crucial to the health and safety of livestock, as minimal blood loss was imperative during procedures such as dehorning and castration; otherwise, the animals in question became weak, sickly, or died.[4] And since these animals were used as food supply *and* for labor, their health was of major concern.

That wasn't all. Farmers soon noticed a lunar connection to their crops as well. It seemed that planting particular crops during specific phases of the Moon brought

---

4. While stock farmers still use these rules of thumb today, this information may have provided the first inkling that the Moon controlled the tides of the human body as well. In fact, it applies to human surgical procedures. Scheduling a personal surgery during the Waning Moon not only increases the chances of a smooth procedure and quick recovery, but lessens the risk of swelling, bruising, and infection.

healthier plants and higher yields. Bulb and root crops, for example, seemed to produce more when planted during the Full to Waning Moon. On the other hand, crops that reseeded themselves did much better when planted during the Dark to Waxing Moon. Plants that produced seedpods and berries provided a higher yield when planted between the Waxing to Full Moon phases. The biggest revelation, though, came with the discovery that no crop did well when planted during the downhill slide of Waning to New Moon. And because of that, early farmers realized that it was an excellent time for weeding, pest control, and other duties they'd previously been too busy to tend. (For further information on lunar gardening, please see chapter 5.)

THE LUNAR METEOROLOGIST

While these discoveries definitely did much to increase crop and animal yields—something that the early peoples relied upon for survival—the Moon was just beginning to reveal Her mysteries, and it wasn't long before something of equal importance came to light. Simply put, the Moon proved to be a fairly accurate predictor of the weather. Since scientific theory hadn't come into play yet, this must have seemed more than just a little remarkable to early humankind. In fact, it's a safe bet that they thought it was real magic in the making.

While it's difficult to differentiate between exactly what ancient civilizations learned about lunar weather forecasts and what came several centuries later, one thing is for sure: the Moon has long served as one of the most definitive tools of weather prediction, and still does today. It's a well-known fact, for example, that more tornadoes and hurricanes occur during the periods of New and Full Moon than at any other time. It's also common knowledge that it tends to rain more often during both the Moon's first quarter and the Waning Moon's first week.

If weather prediction piques your interest, just pay a little attention to the Moon and the symbols that surround Her. With some keen observation and a bit of practice, you can learn to outdo even your favorite television meteorologist. The weather-related Moon adages below will get you started.

★ Pale Moon doth rain, red Moon doth blow, white Moon doth neither rain nor snow.

★ When Full Moon's shadow fills the Crescent, fair weather comes to king and peasant.

★ When a circle appears around the Moon, snow or raindrops will fall soon.

★ Should a ring around the New Moon be, expect disasters out at sea.

★ Should a red Moon rise with large clouds nearby, a half-day brings rain from the sky.[5]

---

5. "Half-day" should be interpreted here as a twelve-hour period.

★ If October's Full Moon brings no frost, none comes till the next Full Moon is tossed.

★ The closer New Moon's arrival to Christmas Day, the longer the Winter stays to play.

★ When the Crescent bears sharp pointed horns, a tempest of the winds is born; but should the horns be blunt and dull, fair weather stays at least till Full.

FEMININE MYSTERIES

As mysterious as all of this must have seemed to the ancient people, one thing definitely topped the list as extraordinary, and this was, of course, the direct connection between the monthly menstrual cycles of women and the comings and goings of the Moon. And while this may not appear to hold much importance in today's world, such was not the case in ancient times. Why? Because these civilizations not only valued their women, but considered them to be extremely magical. The reason is simple but multi-fold. First, women not only bled every month even though they weren't injured, but those who lived and worked together usually bled at the same time.

Second, the temporary suspension of a young woman's cycle brought forth new life. And though this was magical in and of itself, there was more. It soon became apparent that human pregnancy was the only gestation period calculated solely by lunar cycles—nine of them to be exact—and the realization that human beings were the only "lunar primates"[6] served to solidify the connection between the Moon and humankind.

Third and most mysterious, though, was the magic created by older women. Their menstrual cycles suddenly changed course to coincide with the Waning Moon, and shortly thereafter—even though they weren't pregnant—they simply ceased to bleed at all.

In today's world, these observations are nothing more than common knowledge, but to early civilization they must have seemed very peculiar, indeed. In fact, these pieces of knowledge probably served as the catalysts that sparked the initial worship of the Moon in the feminine forms of Maiden, Mother, and Crone.

LUNAR FOLKLORE

If the Moon is feminine in nature, how did we ever come up with the "man in the Moon?" Even though this idea is often thought of as strictly an American invention, such is not the case. The Sanskrit word for moon is "mas," which gives it a masculine form, and etymologists have long debated over whether the same is true of the earliest Teutonic languages. Be that as it may, the concept of the Moon's masculinity is rooted in several ancient mythologies. Khensu, for example, is a Moon-god worshipped by the Egyptians, while Sin belongs to the Baby-

---

6. "Lunar primate" is a term first coined by Z. Budapest in *Grandmother Moon,* published in 1991 by HarperCollins, New York.

lonians. Chandra—a Hindu Moon-god—commandeers a silver chariot drawn by deer with antelopelike antlers as he races across the sky. And, of course, there's also Yue-lao, Chinese mythology's Old Man in the Moon, who predetermines the marriages of unsuspecting humans. It's said that he firmly binds future mates with an invisible silk thread—a thread so strong that nothing can break it but death.

In other areas of the world, though, the Moon's gender takes a back seat to the roles She plays: those of sanctuary, savior, and bringer of swift justice. For example, in Siberia, the residents insist that the figure on the Moon is that of a girl who's been whisked away from the impending danger of an attacking wolf. Scandinavians see two children rescued from a mean and hateful father. His crime? He forced them to carry buckets of water all day.[7]

One of the most interesting Moon myths belongs to the Masai of Kenya. They say that the Sun once severely beat His wife, the Moon. To remind Him of His trespasses—and embarrass Him thoroughly—She consistently shows Her blackened eye and swollen lip to all She encounters.

And then, of course, there's the legend of the Moon Maiden who collects the dreams and wishes of every living creature on Earth. It's said that She tosses these into a

---

7. Many folklorists believe that this Scandinavian myth was the basis for the nursery rhyme "Jack and Jill."

silver goblet and spends the night swirling them together before sprinkling them back on the Earth in the form of dew. In this way, nothing important is ever lost or forgotten. Like everything else, it only changes form.

Other lunar myths seem to concern themselves more with deities who either live on the Moon, or are in charge of its phases. One such myth concerns the Germanic goddess Holle—sometimes called Frigg—who lives on the Moon and busies Herself with spinning the lives of humankind. Another tells of the Chinese goddess Chango, whose husband was given a potion containing the key to immortality. Wanting the gift for herself, the story goes that Chango stole the potion, sucked down every drop, and then flew to the Moon to escape her husband's wrath. It's said that she now lives there happily with the resident hare who gave her refuge.

Then there's another bit of folklore that has nothing to do with gender or deity at all. Instead, it speaks of the ten-day period following the appearance of the Full Moon. It's said that each of these days holds a magic all its own, and that those who pay heed to the individual attributes and use them as prescribed below can expect to become very powerful, indeed.

First Day: This is an excellent time to begin new projects and get new businesses off the ground. It's also an especially lucky day for babies to be born, as these children are said to live exceptionally long, healthy, and prosperous lives. In fact, the only downside to this day at all has to do with illness, as becoming sick now apparently results in an extremely lengthy recuperation period.

Second Day: There is absolutely nothing unlucky about this day; in fact, it vibrates toward riches of all sorts. This is an exceptional time for both merchandise sales and bargain-hunting, and crops and gardens are also said to thrive if planted now.

Third Day: This is not a good day to be born, for it's believed that the children in question are not only likely to be weak, frail, and sickly, but will remain so throughout their lives. Personal theft also seems to make the rounds today. The only upside is that thieves are more likely to be caught in short order—but whether they'll be caught with your belongings is anybody's guess!

Fourth Day: If you're planning to make repairs to your property or redecorate or remodel your home, now is the time to do it. In fact, this day bodes well for anything having to do with building or construction. It's also said that children born on this day are very likely to embrace political careers, but that early training, especially regarding the difference between right and wrong, is imperative to their future successes.

Fifth Day: Known as the "weather marker," it's said that the rest of the month will mirror today's weather. My sources also tell me that this is the best day of the month to conceive a child. I don't know whether this is true or not; however, if babies aren't high on your priority list, a bit of extra precaution might be in order here!

Sixth Day: This is a great day to kick back, relax, and do something nice for yourself. And since it bodes well for making memories, a vacation begun today could prove to be the most fun-filled ever. It's also said to be a very lucky day for hunting, fishing, and outdoor sports of all types.

Seventh Day: Apparently, opportunities simply abound for finding that perfect mate today. So, if you're unattached and looking, get out there and see what this day has to offer. You've got nothing to lose, and you might just get lucky!

Eighth Day: Be very careful of your health today, for it's believed that those who get sick today may not recover, and those who do are likely to be exceptionally weak for some time.

Ninth Day: If you want to keep your good looks, don't gaze upon the Moon today. In fact, you might want to sleep in a totally darkened room, for it's said that if any of tonight's moonlight touches your face, the Moon will certainly steal away all of its beauty.

Tenth Day: Patience is the keyword here, especially when dealing with children born on this day. They're not only said to be hyperactive, opinionated, and headstrong, but may lack even so much as a shred of respect for any sort of authority.

LUNAR SUPERSTITION

Anything of power, especially something with a mysterious power that we don't fully understand, is bound to be surrounded by superstition. And the Moon is certainly no exception. In fact, the Moon is probably shrouded in more superstition than any other object in the Universe.

While some of the following superstitions do actually bear a shred of truth—you're apt to catch more fish by day during the Waning Moon, for example, because fish can see food better in bright light—some of those connected to the Moon are just plain ridiculous. And it's interesting to note that most of the absurdities were largely contributed by leaders of the early church. But why would they even bother to concoct such nonsense? The answer is simple: by making people afraid of the Moon, they hoped to stamp out lunar worship. Naturally, it didn't work. In fact, it only served to add to Her mystique, and increase the interest of nearly everyone She managed to touch with the iridescence of Her silvery light.

Beauty

★ Women should always take care not to let the Moon shine on their faces while sleeping. Otherwise, the Moon will twist their faces and steal their beauty away.

Birth and Pregnancy

★ Pregnant women who sleep with the Moon shining on their bodies will be "moonstruck" and thus give birth to idiots.

★ Should a child be born during the Waning Moon, the sibling who follows shall be of the opposite sex.

★ Should a child be born during the Waxing Moon, the sibling who follows shall be of the same sex.

★ A child born between the phases of the Waning Moon and the New Moon is sickly, weak, and shall not live long.

Devil

★ The devil lives on the Moon and controls Her; thus, he is sure to molest those who gaze upon Her face and claim them as his own in short order.

Fence Building

★ To build a wood fence that will not break or rot, always set the posts while the Moon is waning, and wait until the Moon's horns point skyward to lay the lower rail. Then stake and complete the fence when the Moon's horns point to the Earth. It's said that preparing the fence as such will prevent escape—even the escape of children!

Fishing

★ In the Waxing Moon, set hooks at night; when the Moon doth wane, fish by daylight.

Home Building

★ House foundations laid when the Moon is black will sink into the earth.

★ Only shingle a roof when the Moon is dark; otherwise the shingles will warp.

Livestock

★ Livestock born during a Waning Moon will be sickly and die within the month.

Luck

★ Bow to the Moon when She is new; your luck will then run fast and true.

★ It is unlucky to view a New Moon through tree branches.

★ Pointing at the Moon brings bad luck, but to do so at the first New Moon of the year brings nothing but twelve months of sorrow.

Weddings

★ For a fortunate marriage, set the date twenty-four to forty-eight hours after the appearance of the Full Moon.

★ The Scottish believe that weddings should always occur during the Full Moon to ensure the long-term happiness of the couple.

Wood-Cutting

★ Always cut wood on the Waning Moon, as it's said to prevent damage by termites and worms, and to provide a more slow-burning fire.

THE MOON AND MAGICAL MANIFESTATION

Anything surrounded by centuries of mystery and superstition takes on a very magical quality, and such is certainly the case with the Moon. But has She always been considered a source of enchantment? More to the point, though, is the Moon really magical? Is the power that She seems to hold more than just a simple illusion created in the mind's eye?

While the real answers to these questions are certainly anybody's guess, I believe that a consultation with the Earth's earliest inhabitants would probably bring a positive response to all three questions. For all the advancements we've made in both education and technology through the ages, I also believe that those answers would still be affirmative if posed to today's practitioners. Why? Because anyone who's worked with the Moon in any way, shape, or form simply cannot deny Her power when it comes magical manifestation.

However, I'm also of the opinion that over time, we as practitioners have given the Moon more power than our predecessors ever thought possible. How? Because we've fertilized Her with praise, fed Her with worship, and tended Her with devotion. We've offered Her our deepest emotions, called out to Her in times of need, and depended upon Her light for comfort. We've given Her our energy, and in doing so we've breathed life into Her, charged Her magic, and given Her a potency unsurpassed by any other planet in our system. Because of this, the Moon often seems to have a life of Her own—and even, some might say, a mind of Her own.

Before your eyebrows shoot up in surprise, understand that this isn't necessarily a bad thing. By giving the Moon our energy and strengthening Her power, we've built a very magical creature, indeed. She's become a friend with whom we can bond, a confidante with whom we can share our deepest secrets. And because of Her natural pull upon our emotional makeup, She's also become the strongest ally possible when it comes to practicing the ancient arts.

Like everything else in our world, though, there is another side to this coin. Because we've energized the Moon, we have to be respectful of Her power and use it wisely. This means that we need to think long and hard before we invoke it for magical use. We need to be specific in our intentions. We need to be absolutely certain that our goals are in the best interest of all concerned. Above all, we need to maintain control and direct Her power. Otherwise, the end result of our magic may be anything but that which we first envisioned. In fact, it could take on a life of its own, and that's a place we simply don't want to go.

2

Sheer Lunacy

My dad loved the night sky. We'd sit on the front porch, just the two of us, while he pointed out various constellations and told their stories. He was rather fond of the Moon, too, and it was from him that I first learned of Her cycles and Her power. Of course, I didn't realize at the time that the Moon held any "real" magic. You see, my father wasn't a magical practitioner as such; he was a police officer who raised livestock and liked to garden.

That being the case, my first lessons in "Moon magic" were of a practical nature. I learned the proper phases for planting, thinning, and weed pulling. I was taught when to schedule surgical and dehorning procedures for animals. I was even taught the proper Moon phases for hunting and fishing. But the most important lesson I learned from him, perhaps, had to do with his law enforcement experience. Simply put, it was this: Even the most perfectly grounded person in the world can lose all common sense when the Moon is full.[1]

---

1. This phenomena is the basis for the words "lunatic" and "lunacy."

The reason for this change in behavior is because the Moon controls much more than the tides in our bodies and on our planet; she also controls the emotions, therefore human emotion reaches its peak during the Full Moon. Not convinced? Well, I wasn't either until my father showed me a National Law Enforcement survey back in the early seventies. While I no longer have the exact figures in hand (that was more than thirty years ago) the gist of it was this: Approximately 70 percent of all folks who suffer from mental illness have severe episodes during the Full Moon, and about half of that number eventually wind up in mental institutions or treatment centers. Nearly 80 percent of the crimes committed in any given place in the world are perpetrated at that time as well, and most of these crimes are driven by the rawest emotions in the human makeup: jealousy, rage, depression, and fear. Of course, there's an upside, too. Since the Moon tugs on the emotions in ways completely beyond all human comprehension, more people also fall in love. And there's definitely something to be said for that!

THE MAGICAL CONNECTION

But what does any of this have to do with magic? Everything! Even though the Moon is a part of our everyday lives, She's always been surrounded by a certain amount of mystery. Unlike Her counterpart, the Sun, She's capable of changing form and shape, seemingly at will. She also has a hypnotic quality that often makes Her appear other than She really is. We've all, for example, seen a

Moon so big and bright that we felt we could reach right out and touch it, yet we knew we couldn't. And more than likely, that inherent ability to mesmerize and captivate humankind is at least partially responsible for the Moon's association with the magical realm.

More important, though, is the Moon's connection to the emotions. Because emotion is the matrix from which all successful magic flows—and the Moon evokes strong emotional responses that are completely independent of all logical thought—the Moon is a very valuable tool when it comes to magic. In fact, performing magical operations in conjunction with the Moon is a little like filling a car with gas. Even though everything's in perfect working order, it has to have fuel to get it started and push it down the road. That's what the Moon does for magic; it provides the catalyst necessary to get our spells off the ground.

Since the Moon does affect the emotions so strongly, though, it's important that you, as the practitioner, learn to exercise some emotional control. Otherwise, these emotions—that same wonderful substance that fuels magic and sends it soaring into the Universe—can fly off helter skelter and bring manifestation in ways you hadn't planned. In fact, it can bring magic to fruition even without a formally executed spell. I know what I'm talking about here because it happened to me.

Many years ago, I decided that my black Lab, Sadie, was in dire need of some training, so I boarded her with a man who could do the job. The result was not what I expected. After three weeks, the trainer told me in no uncertain terms that my dog was not only untrainable, but completely incorrigible.

Of course, this was a complete surprise to me. He was, after all, speaking of the same dog who'd been house-trained in two days and taught to sit in a matter of minutes. But I reasoned that this man was the trainer and knew what he was talking about. There was nothing left for me to do but pick Sadie up, take her home, and figure out a way to sort through the problems by myself.

Help often comes in unexpected ways, though, and such was the case with Sadie's training. I received a phone call later that day from a fellow archer. And during the course of the conversation, I discovered that he not only trained Labs, but had five of his own. Even better, they lived in his house, and he was more attached to them than most folks are to their children. It was just the sort of training atmosphere I wanted for Sadie, and before it was said and done, he'd agreed to work with her.

With Sadie back in training and making progress, I decided to leave town for a Full Moon ritual. And it was while I was on the road that I got a call from her new trainer. Apparently Sadie had developed a fear of the training dummies. I couldn't believe my ears. Those little canvas-wrapped tubes had always been her favorite toys, yet her fear was such that she not only hid under the bathroom sink to avoid them, but resorted to an uncontrollable fit of trembling.

Of course, it didn't take long for me to figure it out. The previous trainer, quite frustrated by Sadie's refusal to respond appropriately, had beaten her with one. And with that realization came a fury so irrepressible and uncontainable that I've never again experienced its like. Then the visuals took over. I mentally constructed literally thousands of punishments befitting the crime—all of them horrible, slow, and excruciatingly painful—and visualized each in full detail.

Finally, I managed to clear my mind and pull myself together. Charges this serious called for mundane handling, and since I ran an animal shelter I knew who to call. I decided to have the man's training facility investigated just as soon as I returned; I'd see what transpired and go from there. It was a simple solution designed to bring the desired results.

Except for one thing: It was already too late. The next phone call brought the news.

It was my then-mate and he was babbling excitedly. I only managed to catch the first trainer's name, something about a truck, and a very nastily delivered, "What the hell did you do to him, Dorothy?" Once I got him to slow down, the gist of the conversation was that the previous trainer had just been hit by a truck. The good news? He wasn't dead. The bad news (or other good news, depending on how you looked at it) was that he'd be incapacitated for a while and wouldn't be able to train any more dogs for at least three months.

To say I was dismayed was an understatement; I was shocked beyond belief. Who'd have thought that the very first horror I'd imagined not only would manifest, but manifest along with every minute detail I'd managed to construct? It was almost too much to fathom.

Needless to say, that episode delivered a lesson I won't soon forget. Left unchecked, even for a moment or two, emotions can take on a life of their own. And once they do, nothing can keep them from magical manifestation. Not calmness. Not mundane action. Not even good old-fashioned common sense. The magic is already soaring into the Universe, and any effort to call it back is a futile one, indeed.

EMOTIONAL MANAGEMENT

That's all well and fine, but how do you keep your emotions in check? Is there any way to handle them without becoming completely disassociated from reality or losing all sense of human compassion?

Absolutely. But it won't happen overnight. It takes time, practice, and hard work. Fact is, you have to train yourself to think before you allow any sort of action to take place, even on the mental plane; and that can be difficult, especially if you're as emotionally-driven as I am. Because the alternative is unpleasant, to say the least, I urge you to try the following tips—and do whatever else may be personally necessary—to grab control of your emotions. Otherwise, you'll find your magic controlling you instead of the other way around. And that's a place you simply don't want to go.

Remove all silver jewelry. As the metal of the Moon, silver is directly linked to the emotional realm. But that's not all. It's also one of the strongest energy conductors available to humankind. This means that silver can power the emotions far past their normal capacity. And while that can be very beneficial to magic, it's simply not conducive to good emotional management or clear-headedness. You can always put it back on once you've gotten things back under control.

Focus. No matter what the circumstances, will yourself to look at the problem calmly and with an objective eye. It often helps to ground and center. Just breathe in through your nose, and inhale the green, calming, stabilizing energy from the Earth. Exhale that red, unsettling energy through your mouth, blowing it back into the ground. Three or four repetitions usually does the trick.

Think. Mentally explore every possible solution. Turn the situation around in your mind and look at it from all angles. You may just discover that the best way to handle the problem is mundane in nature, and that magic isn't necessary at all.

Listen. Not just to the advice of friends and family, but to that inner voice as well, because brushing it aside is just asking for trouble. Why? Because it's often that inner voice speaking for the Higher Self that brings the answers you seek.

Once you're back in charge and thinking clearly again, weigh all the options, then make an intelligent decision and take action. It's the best way I know to keep things under control and to manifest your desires without any unpleasant surprises—the latter of which we can all do without!

THE PSYCHIC CONNECTION

While the Moon definitely affects the emotions, there's another area that She impacts just as strongly, and that, of course, is the psyche. I never realized just how true this was until an uncomfortable situation with one of my friends— a woman with an overwhelming amount of psychic ability—presented itself early one morning at Full Moon.

She'd arrived in tears and was desperate for some sort of relief. She said she'd always been a little spacey and had learned to deal with it, but what was happening now was entirely different. Things were out of control. Her whole life seemed to have whirled into a constant flash of kaleidoscopic images, fragmented sounds, and tidbits of information she didn't understand. Not only could she not stop it, she couldn't even slow it down. In fact, things had become so bad that she couldn't even manage one solid thought. Not being able to live like that any longer, she'd come to me for help.

At first, I missed the point. I suggested that she remove her silver jewelry, but it didn't help. We tried grounding and centering. It didn't work. I led her through guided meditations, relaxation exercises, and everything else I could think of, all to no avail. She simply could not focus, not even while holding a hematite in her hand.

I was dumbfounded. In all my years in the Craft, there had never been something I couldn't fix. I knew that every problem, no matter how big or small, had an equally powerful solution. It was just a matter of looking at the problem from every angle and refusing to ignore any detail. With that in mind, I sat down to think. Sure enough, both the problem and its solution eventually became crystal clear.

Her emotional responses, the very things I'd been focusing on, really had little to do with the actual problem. In fact, they were nothing more than a by-product of the real issue. This woman was not only an empath, but had amazingly powerful psychic centers, the latter of which grabbed data in much the same way that a magnet draws nails. And even though she'd reached the capacity to contain it all, those informational tidbits just kept coming—fast and furious, increasing in number and size—until she'd gone on overload.

Why this had never happened to her before is anybody's guess, but what I did learn is this: The amount of data flowing to the psychic centers and the rate of speed at which it travels increases in direct proportion to the size of the Moon. This means that the more the Moon grows, the more information we receive. It just keeps flowing in, steady and constant, until the Full Moon has come and gone.

Once the Moon begins to wane, so does the influx of information. It's almost as if the psychic centers close their doors and refuse to admit anything but the most urgent messages. Things dwindle to a slow crawl until the transmissions stop completely. Then the whole collection just sits there in storage and waits until we're ready to access, process, and sort through it. This usually occurs at the dark of the Moon.

This isn't to say that we can never access psychic information before the Moon is dark, though; nothing could be further from the truth. Messages that are vitally important to our existence or someone else's always push through to the surface; it's just that the psyche isn't able to fully process everything at once. There must be some time to regroup and regenerate—a settling down period, if you will. And that's exactly what the Dark Moon provides.

For most of us, this isn't a problem. In fact, we're often completely unaware of the process. This isn't true for everyone, though, and for those few, it can present more than just a minor aggravation. The inability to regroup and regenerate can result in loss of sleep, poor health, and severe depression. But that's not all. It can also make it extremely difficult to separate reality from fantasy. And that's just no way to live—especially for the magical practitioner.

So what do we do? Is there any way to keep an overflow of psychic messages from sending us off the deep end? More to the point, can we prevent the overload entirely? Absolutely. And it's not as difficult as you may think.

Of course, the best time to handle any situation is *before* it gets out of control, and since psychic overload is no exception, you may want to perform the following ritual before the Moon begins to wax again. That way, you can stop the problem before it ever gets started.

But what if it's too late for that? What if things are already running amuck? What then? Not to worry. Just do the ritual anyway. Even though you may not be able to fully ground, or even completely relax, it will drain the excess psychic energy so you can get through to Dark Moon. Once it arrives, just perform the ritual again and your problems with psycho-babble will be a thing of the past.

Psychic Control Ritual

Materials
1 white candle
1 small piece of hematite
Nagchampa, sandalwood, or dragon's blood incense

Begin by lighting the incense and the candle, then pick up the stone and hold it in your dominant hand. Stand with your feet apart, and raise your arms until they are even with your shoulders, forming a star. With the left palm up and the right palm facing the floor, breathe in the grounding energy of the Earth and exhale any scattered energy through your mouth. Continue to breathe in this fashion until you're totally relaxed. (Three to four breaths usually does the trick.)

Visualize a small opening in your back at the same height as your navel. The opening doesn't hurt or bleed or keep your body from functioning in any way; it's simply there as a safety valve to release psychic overflow should it occur.

Once the image is firmly fixed in your mind's eye, focus on the candle and its light. Feel the light beginning to flow through you and say something like:

I open myself to the Cosmic Light
It flows through my body, both warm and bright

It flows through my psyche and filters through all
And keeps what's important enough for recall
The rest it grabs up as it flows on its way
Draining it off through the valve that I've made
Dissolving its energy—relieving its force—
Returning it to its original source
Then the light of the Cosmos continues to flow
Still protecting my psyche and body from woe

Place the stone in front of the candle and leave it until the flame burns out, then carry the stone with you on a constant basis.

While psychic control is enough of a problem to warrant its inclusion here, it may never cross your path. In fact, your predicament may be just the opposite. It may be that you want to develop your psychic skills more than anything else in the world, but no matter what you do the messages simply refuse to come.

This can be disconcerting, to say the least, especially when everyone else around you seems to be receiving more messages than they care to deal with. After a while, you may even start to think there's something wrong with you. Feelings of inadequacy set in. Anxiety takes over. And before you know it, your mind is so filled with garbage that you wouldn't even recognize your own name if someone screamed it in your ear. If this sounds familiar, I have three words for you.

Stop right there.

To start with, there's nothing wrong with you, and beating yourself up with imagined failure isn't going to fix things. In fact, it could be that you're already receiving psychic messages but just don't know it because psychic information doesn't necessarily arrive in the form we imagine. It seldom comes in some mysterious voice that echoes in the back of the brain. Instead, it's more like a fleeting thought, so we usually just brush it aside and go about our business.

If you're already paying attention to your inner voice, though, there could be other problems. For one thing, your psychic centers may be clogged. It's also possible that you're so grounded you simply don't hear anything other than messages relating to the mundane. If you suspect that one of these issues is the culprit, just try the ritual outlined below. It will not only open the channels, but will put you well on the way to developing those skills you only dreamed of.

Psychic Centers Opening Ritual

Materials
1 purple candle
1 teaspoon dried mugwort or powdered cinnamon
1 small piece of clear quartz, opal, or orange calcite
Nagchampa, sandalwood, or dragon's blood incense
Vegetable oil

Begin by anointing the candle with the oil and rolling it in the mugwort or cinnamon. Light the candle and the incense, then ground and center by breathing in the grounding energy of the Earth and exhaling all other energy through your mouth. Continue to breathe in this fashion until you're totally relaxed. Hold the stone to your Third Eye (the spot between your eyebrows) and visualize it as being the key that opens your psychic centers. See it turn in the lock and watch the doors swing open.

Place the stone in front of the candle, then stand with your feet apart and your arms raised even with your shoulders to form a star. With the left palm up and the right palm facing the floor, continue to breathe in through your mouth and out through your nose for three or four more breaths. Then visualize your psychic centers in perfect working order—receiving and processing messages—and say something like:

> *Psychic centers open wide*
> *So messages can flow inside*
> *Give them voice that I can hear*
> *Let them ring out loud and clear*
> *But let them come through gradually—*
> *No more than my capacity*
> *To understand and handle all*
> *The messages that come to call—*
> *And safety valve, now open too*
> *So psychic overflow won't stew*
> *And grow into anxiety*
> *As I will so mote it be*

Leave the stone in front of the candle until the wick extinguishes itself. Place the stone in a safe place and use it whenever you need a link to the psychic world.

3

Moon Phases and Their Magic

Even though we usually associate the Full Moon with magic, it's not the only phase that tugs at our emotions. The waxing, waning, and dark phases also come into play. In fact, each phase exudes a particular and separate type of energy that feeds and energizes the emotional pool, and since pure, raw, and unadulterated emotion triggers successful magic, the Moon—in all Her phases—comprises one of the most powerful tools we can use in our efforts.

The trick here is to work in harmony with the Moon's phase. Take a spell to gain new friends, for example. Since you're obviously looking to increase the number of people you know (and solidify your moral support system), you'd want to perform the effort when the Moon is waxing or growing in the sky from new to full. But what if the Moon is waning and you don't want to wait several weeks for the proper phase? Not a problem. Just rework the spell to reflect the eradication of your loneliness. You get the idea.

With the exception of the Void of Course Moon, nearly any effort can be performed successfully no matter what the Moon is doing. (For more information, please see "A Moon Without Magic," on page 46.) It's just a matter of knowing the energies of the phase at hand and understanding how to apply them to your cause. Explanations of the Moon phases, their magical correlations, and the Goddess archetypes Who claim them follow below.

WANING MOON

This period belongs to the Dark Maiden and occurs when the Moon shrinks from full to dark, but it doesn't mean that Her power is ebbing. In fact, it's the perfect time to perform efforts that require any sort of shrinkage, elimination, or separation. Good candidates might include weight loss, poor health, debt relief, a gradual separation from damaging relationships, the termination of a bad habit, or the removal of some annoyance from your life. No matter the problem, getting rid of it is easier when the Moon is going down.

What some practitioners don't realize, though, is that the Waning Moon really packs a wallop during its first three to seven days. This period, which occurs just after the Full Moon, is commonly known as the Disseminating Moon, and is excellent for problems that require a complete and final ending. Therefore, work that involves divorce, complete eradication of an addiction or serious health problem, or personal closure of some sort is very effective at this time.

DARK OR NEW MOON

The Dark or New Moon is frequently the subject of heated debate among magical practitioners. So much so, in fact, that there are only three things that practitioners seem to agree upon when it comes to this phase:

1. It occurs during the period between the Waning and Waxing phases.

2. It belongs to the Crone.

3. Even though the Moon isn't visible in the sky, She's still there bathing us with Her energy.

Because of this, the magical practices associated with this phase are as varied and diverse as the practitioners themselves. Many folks, for example, use this phase to rest and relax, regroup and regenerate. Others find this energy extremely useful for delving into past lives, divinatory efforts, magical study, and meditation. A personal favorite for Dark Moon energy, though, is truth discovery. Nothing surpasses its energy for getting to the heart of things and seeing them for exactly what they are.

Still others divide this phase into two parts: New Moon energy and Crescent Moon energy. New Moon energy is afoot from the first day of the Dark Moon to three and a half days after, and is said to be excellent for efforts involving self-improvement, gardening, employment solutions, and health. Crescent Moon energy picks up the slack after that, and is said to continue from the three and a half day mark through the seventh day after the Dark Moon. And those who work with its energy usually harness it for efforts that involve business dealings, animals, feminine strength, a leveling of emotions, or projects that necessitate change of some sort.

While I certainly don't discount the strength of these two energies, or the fact that they work well for the efforts described, I do have to admit that I have a problem with the mathematical figures from which these phases are derived. For one thing, the practitioner would have to consistently check an ephemeris to determine the exact time of the Dark Moon in order to calculate the first three and a half day period with any sort of precision. For another, the Crescent Moon usually isn't even visible in the sky until about five to six days after the Dark Moon. This, of course, means that the Moon is not yet even a sliver during the first couple of days of calculated Crescent Moon energy; thus, it is not a crescent at all. Most important, though, is this: If the Moon is visible in the sky after the Dark Moon, even a bit, it is growing or waxing, and the Waxing Moon does not belong to the Crone or Her energy. Rather, it is ruled by the Light Maiden.

WAXING MOON

Belonging to the Light Maiden, the Waxing phase occurs when the Moon grows in the sky from new to full, and it's during this period that She gains power. That means it's a good time to perform any efforts that require an increase of sorts, or necessitate momentum. Good candidates include spells that involve a fresh start, increased productivity or efficiency, the addition of something to your life, a victory or recognition of sorts, or good health and well-being. If you need more of something, Waxing Moon energy can provide it.

Just as with the Dark Moon energy, though, things can get a bit sticky here with some practitioners as well. Why? Because they also divide the Waxing Moon phase into two separate portions: First Quarter Moon energy and Gibbous Moon energy. Luckily, this isn't nearly as magically confusing as the Dark/New Moon debate. Simply put, they define the First Quarter energy as that which occurs from seven to ten days after the New Moon, and they apply it to any effort that necessitates increase. While they consider Gibbous Moon energy (which occurs, incidentally, from ten to thirteen days after the New Moon) to be of major magical importance, they use it primarily with only one goal in mind: to instill the attribute of personal patience while waiting for an effort to manifest—something that a magical practitioner can never have too much of!

FULL MOON

The Full Moon is ruled by the Mother Goddess, and contrary to popular belief, Her energy isn't necessarily just a one-day affair. In fact, many practitioners consider it to be full (and use its energy as such) for one day before the calendar date and one day after. This is really good news magically for a couple of reasons. For one thing, the Full Moon can be used for any effort at all, but more importantly, the Moon's energy peaks during this time. This means that any effort performed during the Full Moon is not only charged to the max, but packs a cosmic wallop when released into the Universe. Because of this, most practitioners save this phase for handling difficult or complicated matters, or for efforts that require an extra boost. (For more information about specific Full Moons and their energies, please see chapter 4.)

What about the debates on the phases of the Dark and Waxing Moons? Who's right? Who's wrong? More specifically though, how should practitioners handle the Moon phases in order to achieve the best magical success?

The fact of the matter is, like magic itself, there is no right or wrong. How you handle the energies of these Moon phases and apply their powers is your decision alone. Just remember that magic is designed to make your life easier, not the other way around, so do whatever feels right for you and let it go at that. Remember that you are the magician, the matrix from which all magic flows, and as such, you are at the controls.

OCCASIONAL MOON PHASE MAGIC

There's more to the Moon than meets the eye, especially when it comes to magical operations. There are only twelve months in the calendar year. However, the Moon cycles thirteen times during that period, which means that at least two Moon phases of the same type will appear in the same month several times each year. When the repeated phase happens to be the Dark or New Moon, we call the second occurrence the Black Moon.

Since the repetition of anything only serves to increase its power, the Black Moon is very potent. It's said to unearth mysteries with ease, pare matters down to the bare bones, and shed light on even the most deeply hidden truths.

Therefore, the Black Moon provides an excellent time for soul searching and inner journey work, divination, and the eradication of any self-deception. This phase also provides a good time for drawing up plans for the future. Should you decide to work toward a new beginning at this time, though, know that all plans made will reflect the absolute truth, so it's not a good idea to brush aside your inner voice. Listen when it speaks, for while under the power of the Black Moon, it cannot lie.

While the Black Moon is definitely important when it comes to magic, there is another phase that many practitioners revere even more. They believe it's the most powerful of all Full Moon phases, and because it only transpires every couple of years, they await its arrival with much anticipation and excitement. On the other hand, other practitioners believe that it's no more powerful than any other Full Moon, but enjoy the prospect of the additional energy and opportunity it provides for magical workings. This phase is known as the Blue

Moon,[1] and is the third Full Moon to rise when four Full Moons appear within the same season.

As a magical practitioner, how you perceive this energy and where you apply it is up to you. Remember that belief and personal perception are key elements to magical success. So whether you work toward miracles or simply treat this energy as that of another Full Moon, I'd suggest that you give it all you've got. Why? Because it's been my personal experience that no magic—regardless of its magnitude or its triviality—has ever met with anything other than rapid success during the Blue Moon.

Perhaps the only occasional Moon phase that never meets with a debate as to its power is that of the Lunar Eclipse. To the nonpractitioner this may seem a bit odd, because these eclipses happen much more frequently in the solar calendar than the Blue Moon. In fact, they occur at least once annually, and often two to three times within the same year.

No matter how often it occurs, though, the Lunar Eclipse is a magical event more special than any other. For one thing, it provides a time when the energies of the Moon and Sun connect, and this marriage of sorts brings a balance, an equalization of the male and female polarities if you will, that puts everything back in perspective. Because it brings the light-dark-light concept

---

1. Due to erroneous information reported by James Hugh Pruett in an article called "Once in a Blue Moon" (*Sky & Telescope* magazine, March 1946), many people believe that the second Full Moon to occur in the same month is a Blue Moon.

into full view, it's also a reminder of the birth-death-rebirth cycles, and that's something to which nearly all magical practitioners subscribe.

That's not all. The Lunar Eclipse also brings an indescribable sort of energy to everything in its path; something so strong that it goes beyond the point of all human feeling or description. It's an energy that not only embraces us, but fills our very cores to overflowing—even if only for a few moments. Because of its all-encompassing power, Lunar Eclipse energy can be a bit overwhelming; so much so, in fact, that some practitioners refuse to use its power at all in their efforts. They say that its energy is simply too hard to control.

While I understand where they're coming from, this simply isn't true for me. And it isn't true for most of the practitioners I queried. While Lunar Eclipse energy is definitely potent, it is not at all scattered. It's a balanced, cohesive, emulsification of two opposite energies. It's a little like raw milk. Before it's processed, the cream becomes irrevocably separated from the milk, and try as you may, there's nothing you can do to make it stick to the heavier liquid. But homogenize it and see what happens: Both substances blend together in flawless unison, providing a much stronger and more nutritious drink. Such is the way of the Lunar Eclipse. It homogenizes the energies and allows us to work with both as a single unit.

That having been said, all that's left is the decision of whether or not to use this very special energy. I urge you to try it just once. Why? Because the energy related to this occurrence is so powerful it can bring about events that other Moon phases seldom manage. Simply put, Lunar Eclipse energy brings the impossible to fruition; it can single-handedly manifest real miracles.

Keeping that in mind, I suggest saving especially difficult projects for the Lunar Eclipse. Good ideas might include long-term goals like business ventures, financial planning, or successful career changes, as well as efforts that require balance, harmony, or a meeting of the minds. It's also very potent when it comes to developing personal shields—whether they be psychic in nature, or related to a physical protection against poor health, theft, harm, or danger. Want an entirely new life? This is the time to change your personal reality. Don't discount efforts that involve relationships, partnerships, or matters of the heart, either. However, know that the magical effects will be extremely long-lasting.

A MOON WITHOUT MAGIC

Even though the Moon simply exudes magic and seemingly saturates our lives with it whether we want Her to or not, there are approximately twelve times every month when She is positively incapacitated. It's as if all Her power has been stripped away, and suddenly She seems to have no strength or energy or magic at all. In fact, to the magical practitioner, She has no purpose whatsoever, except, of course, to light our way through the dark of night. It's at these times that the Moon is said to be Void of Course.

To some folks, especially those not well versed in astrological terms, saying that the Moon is Void of Course sounds very silly, indeed. For the fact of the matter is that the Moon is *always* on course, moving steadily through each astrological sign every month. That being the case, Her journey continues like clockwork.

There does, however, come a time when even the Moon needs a little R & R. She needs to kick back, relax, and regroup before moving onward, to take a power nap, if you will. And She grabs that opportunity just before She enters the next astrological sign.

So how do we know when the Moon is out of service, and how long do these periods last?

Void of Course periods are usually calculated by a plethora of complicated mathematical equations and variables that few of us truly understand. Couple that with the fact that the length of these periods varies from several minutes to forty-eight hours, and proper calculations could be very sketchy, indeed. Fortunately, though, we don't have to worry about that. An ephemeris, an almanac, or a calendar with accurate Moon data will provide this information right down to the minute. All we have to do is keep one handy, and we're good to go.

Once we have the Void of Course information for the Moon, what do we, as magical practitioners, do with it? In a word, *nothing!* Fact is, all magical operations seem to run amuck when the Moon is chilling out. It's not that they don't work. They do. It's just that they seldom work as planned. It's as if the Universe is suddenly confused as to the quickest route between point A and point B, and things tend to manifest in such a way that we often wish we'd never set them motion.

Think I'm mistaken? Then try this on for size. A former student of mine once did an abundance ritual during a Void of Course Moon. Her first mistake, of course, was asking for abundance instead of prosperity, for money was what she really needed. But even though I reminded her of both problems—the abundance issue and the Void of Course Moon—she went right on with her plans. And what did she get for her trouble? A lot more than she bargained for!

Whole regiments of gophers, moles, and rabbits took up residence in her garden, and what they didn't eat away from below, huge flocks of blackbirds gobbled up from above. Termites invaded her house. Feral cats chose her garage as a birthing quarters. She wound up with an infestation of sand fleas that even a case of sevin dust wouldn't cure. But that was just the abundant contribution from the animal world. Her troubles had just begun.

Both of her children got sick about the same time she lost her second job. Her budget wasn't well padded and didn't allow for extra medical expenses. And while she was fortunate enough to find another job, the hours were absolutely horrendous, which meant additional child care expenses. So in the final analysis, she was doing little more than paying for the privilege to work a second job. All in all, it was her worst nightmare—times three.

Magical efforts aren't the only things that go awry during this period. Computers and peripherals act up, communications get tangled, and plans don't work out. A sense of stalemate is in the air, and because of it, nothing runs true to form, not even the thinking process. This communication breakdown often results in a temporary but unrealistic view of present circumstances. Acting on much of anything at this time could bring very unexpected consequences, indeed.

That having been said, it pays to follow the Moon's lead when She's Void of Course. Just kick back and relax, and take a bit of well-deserved time for yourself. Read a book, see a movie, or take a leisurely stroll through the park. The Moon will be back on track before you know it, and because you had the good sense to rest as well, you'll be raring to go when She is!

4

Full Moon Magic

Since the power of the Full Moon can be used to boost any type of magic, Her arrival is of major importance when it comes to magical work. It's so important, in fact, that many practitioners actually perform a celebratory ritual to honor Her presence. This ritual is commonly known as the Full Moon Circle or Esbat.

Aside from paying homage to the Moon's power, though, there's a second reason for the event. Simply put, each Full Moon has its own sort of energy, an energy that flavors the ruling month, and this means that certain months are more powerful for working with particular types of efforts. Practitioners use the celebration as a way to draw upon this energy and apply it to their workings.

The Esbat usually includes a formal casting of the ritual Circle and a fair amount of structure. For those of you who enjoy that sort of thing, a sample ritual follows. Because it's very generic in nature, this ritual should be used as a guideline only. Why? Because the Esbat should suit your lifestyle and your purpose. More importantly, since every Full Moon exudes a different energy, you'll want to structure each ritual to reflect the appropriate theme. (For more information on Full Moon themes, see the individual Moon sections, beginning on page 57.)

THE FULL MOON RITUAL

Begin by purifying yourself and the ritual area in whatever fashion is normal for you. Place the Element symbols in their appropriate Quarters. A white candle to honor the Lady should be placed on the altar along with an appropriately scented incense and any necessary ritual tools. Candles in a color appropriate to specific Full Moon energy may be added if you wish. For further information and celebration ideas, see the individual Moon sections. Light the candles and incense, purify and cast the Circle, and call the Watchtower Guardians to guard, protect, and witness the ritual. Move to the center of the Circle, ground and center, then say something like:

> *This is a place not a place*
> *In a time not a time*
> *This Circle is sealed*
> *By the words of this rhyme*
> *And floating in balance*
> *'Twixt both worlds tonight*
> *I shall worship the Mother*
> *And bathe in Her light*

Wait a heartbeat or two, then stand with your arms and legs stretched outward and your palms up. Invite the Mother Goddess into the Circle, saying something like:

> *Mother Goddess of both Moon and Star*
> *Who rules all planets near and far*
> *Who rules the Earth and all within*
> *Who sets the time our lives begin*
> *Who brings us happiness and mirth*
> *Who gives us value and self-worth*
> *With every loving touch She gives*
> *Unto this plane on which we live*
> *Please descend now from above*
> *And touch this Circle with Your love*
> *Please join us in this sacred rite*
> *O Mother, bring Your love and light*

Wait a moment or two until you feel Her presence. (Not to worry! You'll know when She's there.) Then recite the Charge of the Goddess[1] in Her honor:

> *I am the harmonious tune of the songbird*
> *And the laughter of a gleeful child.*
> *I am the bubbling sound of the running brook*
> *And the scent of the flowers wild.*
> *I am the floating leaf upon the breeze*
> *And the dancing fire in the forest glade.*

---

1. There are many versions of the Charge. Mine is inserted here for your convenience, but feel free to use whatever version you'd like.

I am the sweet smell of rains upon the soil
And the rapture of passion when love is made.
I am the germination of seed in the Spring
And the ripening of wheat in the Sun.
I am the peaceful depth of the twilight
That soothes the soul when day is done.
I am found in the twinkling of an aged eye . . .
And found in the birth of a newborn pup . . .
Yes . . . Birth and Growth and Death, am I
I am the gracious Earth, on whom you sup.
I am your sister, your mother, the wise one.
I wrap you gently in the warmth of my love.
That which you seek you shall find within:
Not without . . . not below . . . not above!
Remember always, my children, be reverent
Be gentle, loving, and kind to each other
And hold sacred the Earth and its creatures
For I am the Lady, Creatrix, and Mother!

Wait a heartbeat or two, then ask the Mother to fill your Spirit with the energy of the Full Moon at hand, and help you to understand its lessons. (The following invocation is general in nature. For other invocation ideas appropriate to specific Full Moon Circles, see the individual Moon sections.)

O gracious Goddess of the Moon
Mother of Creation
Please grace me with Your presence now
Accept my invitation

Come from the starry heavens now
As Your Mysteries I embrace
I ask You, Mother, come to me
Descend upon this space

After the invocation, perform any magical work you had in mind. When you're done, hold the cakes in front of you and bless them by saying something like:

I conjure You, O meal of grain
Who sprouted in both Sun and Rain
Whose ancient seed fulfills us all
And gains new life where e'er it falls
I bless You in this Circle round
That Your abundance may abound
And feed our world continuously
As I will, so mote it be

Eat one of the cakes. If this is a group ritual, take a bite, then pass the platter to the person on your left with a kiss and a "blessed be." When the platter reaches the altar again, proceed with the wine or juice blessing by holding the liquid in front of you and saying something like:

I conjure You, O fruit of vine
Who grew with Wind and Rain and time
From nothing but the light of Sun
And light of Moon when day was done
I bless You in this Circle round
That Your abundance may abound
And feed our world continuously
As I will, so mote it be

Pour the liquid into a goblet and take a drink. If this is a group ritual, pass the goblet to the person on your left with a kiss and a "blessed be." When the goblet reaches the altar again, you have one of two options: You may either take some time to visit with each other in Circle, or proceed with closing the ritual. Should you choose the latter, thank the Mother Goddess for attending the ritual by saying something like:

> *Mother Goddess of both Moon and Star*
> *Who rules all planets near and far*
> *Who rules the Earth and all within*
> *Who sets the time our lives begin*
> *Who brings us happiness and mirth*
> *Who gives us value and self-worth*
> *With every loving touch She gives*
> *Unto this plane on which we live*
> *We thank You for Your presence here*
> *And hold You in our hearts so dear*
> *And with our love now, You may go*
> *Or stay, if You should deem it so*

Dismiss the Guardians and release the Circle, then go outdoors and leave some cakes and wine for the animals.

But what if you're not comfortable with that much formality and structure? Can you celebrate the Full Moon without the pomp and circumstance of formal Circle-casting? Absolutely. (The only exception is if you plan to perform some serious protection magic designed to provide a shield from abuse, addiction, impending danger, or invasive disease.) Just outline the Circle area with flowers, leaves, salt, or something else that strikes your fancy, and concentrate on celebrating the Full Moon's arrival and Her importance in your life. All that's really necessary is a simple but heartfelt declaration of honor, an understanding of the energies that each Full Moon provides, and a request for lending Her power toward the efforts at hand. Add a little imagination, and you have a celebration on your hands. The following information will set you on your way.

DECEMBER: THE OAK MOON[2]

Thematic Energy

The energy of this Moon is masculine and, as the name implies, centers around the oak tree and its many magical significances. Since this Moon rises in close proximity to Yule, the battle of the Holly and Oak Kings (symbolizing the Waning and New Years, respectively) comes to the forefront. It's the time when the Oak King claims rulership and brings the returning light and warmth of the newborn Sun with him. But that's not all. The tree for which this Moon is named also has magical value. For one thing, its trunk and branches rise high into the sky while its roots dig so deeply into the Earth that they were

---

2. Since the Full Moon closest to Winter Solstice is commonly known as the Oak Moon, I've begun the Lunar Wheel with the month of December.

once thought to infiltrate the Underworld. This makes it the perfect illustration of equal growth on both the physical and spiritual planes, something that is necessary for personal balance. Then there's the matter of the mistletoe that grows green, lush, and bountifully on the oak's branches, even in the dead of Winter. The white berries that form at this time of year symbolize the semen of the Lord of the Forest, and remind us that life is always new, always fruitful, and always constant.

Magical Efforts
This particular energy is excellent for candle magic that involves strength, self-confidence, balance between the worlds, prosperity, release, and beginnings. It also provides a good time to honor the birth of the Sun.

Sample Oak Moon Invocation
> *O Mother, by Your radiant glow*
> *Into my very Spirit sow*
> *The balancing energy of the Oak*
> *Its fires of birth within me stoke*
> *Bring its strength unto my core*
> *Give wing to confidence—let it soar*
> *And grant its rich prosperity*
> *As I will, so mote it be*

Oak Moon Circle Ideas
★ Dress in shades of white, yellow, and gold to welcome the Mother's newborn Sun.

★ Use white candles on the altar, and burn frankincense-scented incense. Alternatively, burn Full Moon Incense. (For the recipe, see "Full Moon Phase Efforts" in part 2.)

★ Decorate altars with oak leaves, holly, mistletoe, and Sun symbols.

★ Mark the Circle boundary with yellow candles or unsalted sunflower seeds. If you opt for seeds, gather them after the ritual and put some aside for Spring planting. Leave the rest outside for the birds.

★ Serve gingerbread cookies and apple wine for libation. (If you prefer a nonalcoholic beverage, try spiced cider.)

★ For spell work appropriate to this Moon, see "Full Moon Phase Efforts" in part 2.

Oak Moon Party Ideas

★ Decorate with the colors and items suggested in the preceding "Circle Ideas" section.

★ Serve gingerbread or spice cake and hot apple cider as refreshments.

★ If this Moon rises prior to Yule, plan a caroling expedition.[3] (Be sure to check with your local government

---

3. For pagan-oriented lyric ideas, check out:
   http://sanfords.net/Pagan_Humor_and_Thoughts/Pagan_Yule_songs.htm.

first to see whether you need a parade license or other permit.)

★ Give all participants slips of paper and ask them to write down items that they wish to remove from their lives. Then have them toss the papers into a small fire built of oak wood while asking the newborn Sun to replace the unwanted items with items of a more positive nature.

★ Have a gift exchange. Just ask each attendee to bring an inexpensive nongendered gift, then hand out the gifts at random. Have each person tell why the item he or she received is particularly significant. (Since these gifts have a way of going to exactly the right person, it's a safe bet that everyone will have something to say!)

★ Games that require strength and balance are appropriate for this celebration. Good ideas might include indoor relay races where the object is not to spill a glass of water, or maybe even a good-natured arm wrestling contest. Conversational continuity is also fun to play. Just hand out slips of paper marked with words appropriate to the Oak Moon. The first player must end a statement with the word on his or her slip. The next player must begin a statement with the last player's word and end it with his or her own. It's great fun and easily gets the whole group involved.

★ Acorns that have been blessed for strength and courage make great party favors.

JANUARY: THE WOLF MOON

Thematic Energy

This Moon is named for the wolf for two reasons. First, it arrives during the most frozen part of the year—a time when natural food supply levels are at their lowest in woodland areas. This means that wolves and other predators must often venture into towns and other populated areas to satisfy their hunger. Second, and more important, wolves—like humans—are family-oriented. Depending on each other for wisdom, love, and moral support, they cultivate families, live in packs, and remain together throughout life. This sense of togetherness is essential to the wolf's very existence, for without it, the wolf simply pines away from loneliness.

As you celebrate this Esbat, remember that the human species, like the wolf, is also rooted in family structure. Therefore, take a little time to appreciate those closest to you. Spend some time together. If difficult issues are at hand, work toward resolution. Thank family members for the roles they've played in your life, for without them you wouldn't be the person you are today. Remember to spend some time with the Ancients, too; for They are not only family members, They are family members Whom you chose.

Magical Efforts

Wolf Moon energy is particularly helpful in efforts that require sorting through family issues or that seek a renewed bonding of the family unit. The Wolf Moon provides an excellent time to work on relationships, partnerships, and matters of the heart, as well as efforts that involve new ventures or projects that require courage.

Sample Wolf Moon Invocation

> *Mother Goddess, hear my plea*
> *Bring Wolf Moon energy to me*
> *And with it, bring into my heart*
> *That constant love that does not part*
> *From friends or family or those*
> *Who hold me dear—both far and close—*
> *Lend courage as I start anew*
> *Please bring these things, I ask of You*

Wolf Moon Circle Ideas

★ Wear shades of burgundy, pink, or rose to symbolize family love and togetherness. Sweaters in these shades also work well to represent the close-knittedness of family bonds.

★ Use burgundy or rose-colored candles on the altar, and burn an evergreen-scented incense like pine, cedar, or cypress. Alternatively, burn Full Moon Incense. (For the recipe, see "Full Moon Phase Efforts" in part 2.)

★ Decorate the altar with mementoes and souvenirs of special occasions, and photos of family and friends. Incorporate apples as well, for they are the fruit of love.

★ Outline the Circle perimeter with bits of evergreen, then asperge it with a pine branch to symbolize eternal life and growth.

★ Serve sugar cookies and apple juice or cider for libation.

★ For spell work appropriate to this Moon, see "Full Moon Phase Efforts" in part 2.

Wolf Moon Party Ideas

★ Decorate with the colors and items suggested in the preceding "Circle Ideas" section.

★ Serve apple slices with caramel dip, and hot apple cider.

★ Sit in a circle and ask each participant to tell a short story about how a family member or friend impacted their life in a positive way. Alternatively, have each participant say something positive and uplifting about the person to their left.

★ Hold a scavenger hunt. Just divide the participants into teams and have them work together to find the items on their list. Give a small wolf print or statue to the winning group. (If you'd like to make this an annual event, the prize can be passed on from year to year.)

★ Since this is a celebration of togetherness, any group activity can be utilized. Games like Twister or charades are good bets, as are sing-alongs or group dances.

★ Little bags of heart-shaped cinnamon candies make good party favors.

THE STORM MOON[4]

Thematic Energy

Named for the frigid outbursts of Winter that sweep across the land, the Storm Moon brings blankets of ice and snow that insulate the Earth and everything beneath its surface. All is quiet now, for Mother Nature has gone to bed. Resting peacefully, She dreams of the coming Spring, the vibrant colors of flowering bulbs, and the shade of green that can only be attributed to newly sprouting grass. She sleeps deep and long, and as She does Her power supply—a necessary component for the busy growing season that lies ahead—is revived, renewed, and regenerated.

The Storm Moon brings a time of rest and renewal for us, too, so take a little time for yourself. Just kick back, relax, and reenergize. Go deep within yourself and take that inner journey. Discover who you are, where you're going, and who you hope to become. Contemplate your personal reality, your future, and your path. In doing so, you'll not only be ready for your personal growing season, but will have a set of plans to put into place when it arrives.

---

4. Because of the sporadic arrival of the Blue Moon, a second Moon is inserted here for the sake of convenience.

Magical Efforts

This energy provides a good time for efforts that require divination, meditation, and inner journey work as well as those that involve physical energy, health issues, psychism, and prophetic dreaming. It is also very useful in works that require long-lasting effects.

Sample Storm Moon Invocation

> *O Mother Goddess, bring to me*
> *The wondrous Storm Moon's energy*
> *To open up my psychic eyes*
> *That I may cut through all disguise*
> *And see all things with clearest view*
> *Bring its time of rest now, too*
> *So that my strength's renewed with ease*
> *As I will, so mote it be*

Storm Moon Circle Ideas

★ Adorn yourself in soft shades of blue to encourage the resting period of the Earth.

★ Use blue candles on the altar, and burn sandalwood or nagchampa incense. Alternatively, burn Full Moon Incense. (For the recipe, see "Full Moon Phase Efforts" in part 2.)

★ Use a blanket or quilt as an altar cloth, then decorate with paper snowflakes, stars, and other symbols indicative of peaceful dreaming.

★ If casting a formal Circle, use a dream catcher in place of the wand or athame.

★ Serve hot chocolate and butter cookies for libation.

★ For spell work appropriate to this Moon, see "Full Moon Phase Efforts" in part 2.

Storm Moon Party Ideas

★ Decorate with the colors and items suggested in the preceding "Circle Ideas" section.

★ Serve hot chocolate and s'mores as refreshments.

★ Since the Earth is sleeping, the ideal celebration would be an old-fashioned slumber party or indoor camp-out. If that's not possible, plan a party where the only requirement is that attendees show up dressed in their pajamas.

★ Have each attendee make a "coupon" for a mini-divinatory reading of their specialty. Toss the coupons in a sack and let folks draw them at random. Allow everyone to cash in their coupons and get a reading. But what if all your attendees don't do readings? Not a problem. Shoulder massages, foot rubs, and other relaxing amenities work nicely, too.

★ Play "pass the dream catcher." Just form a circle and give one attendee a dream catcher. Then ask that person to tell a short fairy-tale, ghost story, or other bedtime story. Upon conclusion, pass the dream catcher to the next person while he or she tells a story. Continue around the circle.

★ Have a lullaby writing contest. Give the winner a small prize.

★ Give small pieces of tumbled citrine as party favors. These are especially significant if you charge them first for pleasant dreams.

FEBRUARY: THE CHASTE MOON

Thematic Energy

The energy of the Chaste Moon is one of innocence, joy, and purity. It not only speaks to the inner child, but reminds us of a time when life was a simple business with few worries or demands, a time when the imagination came to the forefront, anything seemed possible, and smiles—something seemingly in short supply these days—came quickly and easily. The Chaste Moon awakens childlike fun, jolts the imagination, and begs us to simplify our busy lives.

As the Chaste Moon rises high in the sky, do something fun for yourself, something that you enjoyed as a child. Play, color, or ride the merry-go-round. Simplify your life by weeding out everything that is no longer meaningful or useful. In doing so, you'll discover that obstacles—even those that have long barred your path—will give way to fresh and exciting ideas to bring about goal attainment.

Magical Efforts

This Moon provides the perfect energy for efforts that require simplification, the eradication of that which is old and useless, and the termination of barriers and obstacles. It's also perfect for work involving personal goals, solutions to messy situations, and any type of fresh start or beginning.

Sample Chaste Moon Invocation

> *O Mother, I ask that You now infuse me*
> *With the innocent joy of Chaste Moon energy*
> *Wipe out what is old and bring forth the new*
> *Eradicate boundaries in all that I do*
> *Clarify issues as never before*
> *So solutions are simple; let creativity soar*
> *As goals meet inspiration and I'm all I can be*
> *I ask as Your child, bring this magic to me*

Chaste Moon Circle Ideas

★ Dress in white to honor the childlike joy and innocence of the Chaste Moon.

★ Cover the altar with a white lace tablecloth, and decorate it with white flowers. Any flowering bulbs of the season (narcissus, snow-drops, white hyacinths, or tulips) will work well.

★ Use white candles on the altar and burn a light, floral incense. Alternatively, burn Full Moon Incense. (For the recipe, see "Full Moon Phase Efforts" in part 2.)

★ Forego the "normal" Element symbols and replace them as follows: a pinwheel for Air, cinnamon-flavored candies or a small fire truck for Fire, a basket of seashells or a mermaid doll for Water, and building blocks for Earth.

★ Cast the Circle with a bubble wand and lots of blown bubbles. Outline its boundary with white paper chains if you like.

★ Serve chocolates and hot lemonade, or chocolate chip cookies and milk for libation.

★ For spell work appropriate to this Moon, see "Full Moon Phase Efforts" in part 2.

Chaste Moon Party Ideas

★ Decorate with the colors and items suggested in the preceding "Circle Ideas" section.

★ Serve cookies and milk, or graham crackers with peanut butter and Kool-Aid as refreshments.

★ Play childhood games like jacks, hopscotch, pin-the-tail-on-the-donkey, and musical chairs. Bubble-blowing contests, either with bubblegum or soap bubbles, are fun, too. Just give a little thought to the games you enjoyed as a child and put them on the agenda.

★ Ask everyone to bring a toy to the party, then as a group, take them to a homeless shelter and present them to the children.

★ Give ribbon-tied lollipops as party favors.

MARCH: THE SEED MOON

Thematic Energy

The coming of the Seed Moon heralds the beginning of the growing season, and all of Nature steps in harmony. Bulb sprouts shoot through the Earth and burst into blossoming beauty. Tree branches bud. Squirrels and rabbits frolic in the warmer weather, and birds flit to and fro in search of nest-building materials. Spring has arrived with Her wild and unbridled energy, touching all in Her path with the need to create, play, grow, and flourish.

When this energy comes to call, the last thing you want to do is sit still. That being the case, toss back the covers, get up, and get going. Work in the garden or re-pot your houseplants. Write down ideas, make plans, and start new projects. Creative urges tickle every one of your senses right now. And why shouldn't they? The Seed Moon has come to play, touching all in Her path with the promise of fresh growth and new life.

Magical Efforts

As the name implies, the Seed Moon brings a good time for any preliminary work that involves magical gardening: seed blessings, garden space or tool consecrations, and so forth. But that's not all. It also provides an excellent time for efforts that involve personal growth, creativity, inspiration, and the cultivation of fresh perspective.

Sample Seed Moon Invocation

> *As the Earth is in sprouting mode, Mother so dear*
> *Let me, too, germinate—cast off my fear—*
> *Encourage fresh sprouting in my heart and my soul*
> *So I quickly grow past what is useless and old*
> *And tend the new sprouts of growth and perspective*
> *With fresh inspiration and a creative directive*
> *Fill up my life with Seed Moon energy*
> *For I wish to grow; as I will, it shall be*

Seed Moon Circle Ideas

★ Adorn yourself in shades of green to honor the freshly sprouting Earth.

★ Cover the altar with pale green fabric, and decorate it with wildflowers or forsythia and Spring greenery.

★ Use green candles on the altar, or try white or yellow candles set in leaf-covered candle-rings. Burn a soft, floral incense; alternatively, use Full Moon Incense. (For the recipe, see "Full Moon Phase Efforts" in part 2.)

★ Cast and asperge the Circle with a budding tree branch. After ritual, put this in a safe place. You'll want to keep it to burn in the Beltane Fires.

★ Serve poppy seed rolls or bread sprinkled with sesame seeds, and milk for libation.

★ After ritual, place small piles of colored threads under trees for birds to use as nest-building supplies.

★ For spell work appropriate to this Moon, see "Full Moon Phase Efforts" in part 2.

Seed Moon Party Ideas

★ Decorate with the colors and items suggested in the preceding "Circle Ideas" section.

★ Serve fruit punch and round loaves of seed-sprinkled bread with onion dip and a green onion garnish. Just cut the center from the loaf, fill with dip, and "plant" with onions. This makes a beautiful centerpiece, and it is tasty, too!

★ Have a seed exchange. Ask all attendees to bring a package of easy-to-grow herb or flower seeds that have been blessed or charged for a specific purpose (love, prosperity, protection, wisdom, and so on). Place them in a basket and have each participant select a package without peeking. Folks always manage to get exactly what they need.

★ Garden party barters are fun, too. Folks just bring some gardening-related item they no longer want— flower pots, hand spades, or gloves, for example—and allow others to pay for them by trade of another item or personal services. It's a great way to get rid of things you don't want and acquire some things that you do.

★ Make nest-building containers for the birds. Just cut chicken wire into strips measuring 12 inches by 6 inches and tie the ends of each strip together with ribbon to form circular containers. Then tie eight lengths of ribbon across one open end to form wheel spokes. (This will serve as the bottom and partially close the container.) Fill with pieces of cotton, fiberfill, Easter grass, colored threads, or anything else that the birds might use. Tie ribbons to the top and hang outdoors.

★ Weather permitting, this is also an excellent time to prepare flower beds and gardens for planting. And handled as a group with lots of singing and laughter, it not only saves time but can provide tons of fun for everyone involved. If you do this, though, you'll have to reward your party-goers for a job well done, which means that dinner may be in order.

★ Small pouches of wildflower seeds make great party favors, especially when blessed for wishing purposes. Just instruct your guests to make a wish, then toss the seeds on the winds for manifestation.

APRIL: THE HARE MOON

Thematic Energy

Boundless fertility is the Hare Moon's gift, and She pours it out on all in Her keep. Meadows, lawns, and trees sprout in verdant green. Garden flowers bloom and wildflowers sprinkle hills, valleys, and roadsides. Reproductive urges in animals run high as well, and with the need for family growth at the forefront, all of Nature is happy and busy.

The Hare Moon doesn't just affect the world around us, though. Under Her light, we feel the urge to grow and flourish, too. Our production levels run high both spiritually and physically as we set plans in motion and see where they'll go. We restructure ideas and weed out that which keeps us from reaching our goals. But that's not all. With this particular energy permeating every cell of our being, our thoughts also lean toward romance. In fact, it's been my personal observation that more people fall in love during this time than any other.

Magical Efforts

The fertile energy of the Hare Moon brings a good time for efforts that involve increased physical health, productivity, renewed energy, and the removal of obstacles that keep us from reaching goals. It's also the perfect time for performing any work related to the fey, magical gardening (setting out and consecrating plants and seedlings, and so on), or matters of the heart.

Sample Hare Moon Invocation

> *O Fertile Mother, I now ask of Thee*
> *To fill my life with Hare Moon energy*
> *Please bring productivity and revitalize*
> *My spirit and mind so decisions are wise*
> *I ask for my body a healthy condition*
> *I ask that my goals come at once to fruition*
> *And bring, too, the positive magic of fey*
> *Bring forth this energy, Mother, today*

Hare Moon Circle Ideas

★ Wear soft pastels to symbolize happiness and fertility. Alternatively, dress in soft shades of green, yellow, or peach.

★ Decorate the altar with colored eggs, pictures of rabbits, Spring greenery and flowers, or other symbols of joy and fertility.

★ Use green, yellow, or peach candles on the altar and burn a fruity-scented incense like coconut, peach, or strawberry. Alternatively, use Full Moon Incense. (For the recipe, see "Full Moon Phase Efforts" in part 2.)

★ Cast and asperge the Circle with a bunch of violets or wildflowers tied in pastel ribbons. Scatter the Circle perimeter with wildflowers if you like.

★ Serve sugared violets (violet flowers first dipped in egg white and then in sugar) or lemon cookies and strawberry wine. For a nonalcoholic beverage, serve Kool-Aid.

★ For spell work appropriate to this Moon, see "Full Moon Phase Efforts" in part 2.

Hare Moon Party Ideas

★ Decorate with the colors and items suggested in the preceding "Circle Ideas" section.

★ Serve deviled eggs or egg salad sandwiches, and strawberry Kool-Aid or wine.

★ If children are present, tell the story of Eostre, the Spring goddess, and how the most famous hare of all, the Easter Bunny, came to be.

★ Have an egg-decorating contest. Just boil the eggs, provide some dye and colored markers, and see where the creativity leads.

★ Once the eggs are dry, have an egg hunt. Put special marks on some of the eggs, and provide small prizes to those who find them.

★ Since this is truly a celebration of fertility, it's also a good time for a "prosperity planting." All you need is one uncooked egg for each attendee, a few basil seeds charged for prosperity, some potting soil, and some yarn or ribbon. Using a straight pin or needle, just poke a hole in each end of the eggshell, then blow out the contents. Carefully cut away the narrow end of the egg-shell with sharp scissors and poke three holes around the upper perimeter. Fill with soil, plant with the seeds you've named for prosperity, and spritz with water. Thread knotted lengths of ribbon or yarn through the holes for hanging. Once the seedlings mature, they can be planted in the garden, eggshell and all.

★ Small chocolate bunnies or packages of pastel-colored M&Ms make excellent party favors.

MAY: THE DYAD MOON

Thematic Energy

Signifying the consummation of the marriage of the Lord and Lady, the Dyad Moon is very powerful indeed. At this time, the Couple twirls in perfect synchronization, not only moving across the Earth in a passionate mating dance of sheer ecstasy, but fertilizing all in Their path. Trees and grass grow lush and verdant. Flowers burst into full bloom. The winds and rains give way to the golden rays of the Sun. And the world, once more, basks in the warm glow of fertile sensuality.

With the growing season at its most fertile, the Dyad Moon provides an excellent time for all sorts of creative endeavors. Projects are completed easily now, and new ideas come together cohesively. In fact, it seems that everything, even the wildest dream, is well within the realm of possibility. All we have to do is reach out and grab it!

Magical Efforts

The energy of this Moon is so potent that even the impossible is within reach, so work on difficult problems now. In addition, the Dyad Moon provides an excellent time to perform efforts involving matters of the heart, fertility, passion, physical stamina, energy, health, friendships, prosperity, and completion.

Sample Dyad Moon Invocation

> *O Mother, as You twirl about*
> *In loving dance, the world throughout*

Infuse me with Your energy
Bring to my work, fertility
So all my goals grow lush from seed
And manifest by word and deed
And fill my heart, too, with Your love
As You look down now from above

Dyad Moon Circle Ideas

★ Dress in bright colors and adorn yourself with flowers of the season.

★ Cover the altar with a lace tablecloth, and decorate with wedding paraphernalia and fresh flowers.

★ Use gold and silver candles on the altar, and burn a floral incense like jasmine, orange blossom, or apple blossom. Alternatively, use Full Moon Incense. (For the recipe, see "Full Moon Phase Efforts" in part 2.)

★ Cast and asperge the Circle with a wedding bouquet fashioned of fresh flowers tied with brightly colored ribbons. Use it for a wedding bouquet toss after Circle. If you're celebrating alone, leave the bouquet outside atop the outdoor libation area.

★ Serve white cake and mimosas (champagne mixed with orange juice) for libation. For a nonalcoholic beverage, serve flavored sparkling water.

★ For spell work appropriate to this Moon, see "Full Moon Phase Efforts" in part 2.

Dyad Moon Party Ideas

★ Decorate with the colors and items suggested in the preceding "Circle Ideas" section.

★ Serve finger sandwiches, chips, chocolate covered strawberries, and white cake with mimosas or fruit punch.

★ Celebrate the workings of friendships, partnerships, and intimate relationships. Hand out award certificates to all the attendees. Some ideas might include the award of a certificate to the person who's made the most progress in people skill development, another to the couple with the longest lasting relationship or friendship, and so forth.

★ Ask everyone to bring flowers or herb snippets from their gardens (small bunches of wildflowers picked from the roadside work well, too), and use a book on floriography to discover the messages that each plant delivers. Then make small bouquets to spell out specific messages for each attendee.

★ Even if the Full Moon doesn't arrive close to May 1, this is still a good time to make May baskets. Just form small cones from colored construction paper and use ribbons or yarn to fashion handles, then fill the baskets with leftover flowers, small packages of flower seeds, and a few individually wrapped candies. Hang them on doorknobs throughout the neighborhood.

★ If you're holding the party at night, consider having a dance. Better yet, have a dance contest with several categories and award small prizes to the winners.

★ Small bundles of fertilizer sticks or tulle-wrapped bird seed tied with green satin ribbons and blessed for creativity make excellent party favors.

JUNE: THE MEAD OR HONEY MOON

Thematic Energy

With the rising of the Mead Moon comes the sweetness of new life, metamorphosis, and transformation. Birds hatch, animals give birth, and cicadas and butterflies burst forth in a flurry of excitement. Hives, which only last month were barren, are now laden with honey and ready for harvest. The world is fluxing and flexing with change just now, and all of Nature seems more than happy to comply.

We feel the need for change as well, and this often results in the fresh perspective necessary to start our lives anew. We find it easier to reinvent our lives and become the people we were born to be. Once that happens, our personal realities follow suit, bringing positive life changes we never dreamed were possible, not even in the mind's eye.

Magical Efforts

The metamorphical energy of the Mead Moon provides a perfect time for efforts involving personal transformation, a positive change of life circumstances, or the total reinvention of your life or self. Because it's a very fertile Moon, efforts that involve prosperity, inspiration, and creativity also come to fruition quickly now.

Sample Mead Moon Invocation

> *O Mother Who brings fertile birth*
> *Infuse me with Your joy and mirth*
> *Bring forth my personal transformation*
> *Without a moment's hesitation*
> *Let me become who I should be*
> *And live the life that's meant for me*
> *A fertile life—a verdant one—*
> *Laced with love and warmth of Sun*

Mead Moon Circle Ideas

★ Wear shades of yellow, gold, and amber in honor of the honey harvest.

★ Cover the altar with yellow fabric and use dandelions, cicada shells, shed butterfly cocoons, hatched bird eggs, and shed feathers to decorate.

★ Use yellow, orange, or gold candles on the altar, and burn frankincense and myrrh incense. Alternatively, use Full Moon Incense. (For the recipe, see "Full Moon Phase Efforts" in part 2.)

★ Outline the Circle boundaries with feathers, seashells, or some other transformative gift of Nature.

★ Serve lemon cookies, or lemon pound cake and mead. For a nonalcoholic beverage, serve honey-sweetened tea.

★ For spell work appropriate to this Moon, see "Full Moon Phase Efforts" in part 2.

Mead Moon Party Ideas

★ Decorate with the colors and items suggested in the preceding "Circle Ideas" section.

★ Serve pineapple upside-down cake or cookies made with honey, and mead or honey-sweetened tea.

★ Have a costume party, and ask the attendees to come dressed as the person they eventually hope to become. Also ask them to take on the personas of the newly invented self. Give a small prize to the person who seems to accomplish this task with the most skill.

★ If you go the costume party route, play a game of "What's My Line?" Focusing on one person at a time, have the other attendees ask questions to figure out who or what they've become. Let everybody have a turn.

★ Go on a nature hunt, the object being to find as many transformative gifts of Nature (feathers, hatched egg shells, shed cicada shells, and so on) as possible. Include them in charm bags to help with the personal metamorphical process. Save any leftover feathers for making Witches' Ladders later in the year.

★ Give small beeswax candles or honeycombs as party favors.

JULY: THE WORT MOON

Thematic Energy

Named for the Anglo-Saxon word "wort," which means herb, the rise of this Moon heralds the time of the first harvest. Flowering and fruitful, herbs have reached their full growing potential now. And as their heady aromas waft through the air, they simply beg to be cut and gathered and included in all of our magical and mundane projects.

The Wort Moon signals the beginning of our personal harvests, too. It's a time when we're called upon to put everything we've learned over the past year to good use, and a time when we're not only expected to apply it to spiritual lives, but to our magic. Fortunately, this isn't as difficult as it sounds. Spiritual matters seem to make more sense now. Prophetic dreams come to the forefront, and psychic abilities seem to develop almost by themselves. Even divination comes more easily. Just go with the spiritual flow and give yourself over to the harvest. The benefits that you reap will far outweigh any sacrifice.

Magical Efforts

Because the energy of this Moon speaks of completion and application, all magical efforts meet quickly with success now. Since the emphasis is on the spiritual, though, efforts involving personal psychism, prophetic dreamwork, divination, and reincarnative path-working make especially good candidates.

Sample Wort Moon Invocation

> *As the herbs go to harvest now, Mother above*
> *Harvest my spirit with Your gentle love*
> *Lend both Your courage and Your guiding hand*
> *Direct me and move me so I understand*
> *How to apply all the knowledge You've brought*
> *A step at a time till it's seamlessly wrought*
> *Through my life and my magic—in every direction—*
> *For I am Your harvest and thus Your reflection*

Wort Moon Circle Ideas

★ Dress in shades of orange, green, and yellow to commemorate the herb harvest, and wear wreaths of herbs
or greenery in your hair.

★ Cover the altar with a yellow cloth, and decorate with
ribbon-tied bunches of dried or flowering herbs. After
ritual, leave a few outside for the fairies.

★ Use orange and green candles on the altar, and burn
a mixture of lavender, rosemary, and sage as incense.
Alternatively, use Full Moon Incense. (For the recipe,
see "Full Moon Phase Efforts" in part 2.)

★ Asperge the Circle with a bouquet of herbs or plants
and your favorite herbal tea. Chamomile, lemon balm,
or mint are excellent choices.

★ Outline the Circle area with ribbon-tied herbal sprigs.
After Circle, give one to each attendee for use in his
or her magical efforts.

★ Serve herbal cookies and herbal tea for libation. To make herbal cookies, add a tablespoon of lavender, lemon balm, or mint to your favorite sugar cookie recipe.

★ For spell work appropriate to this Moon, see "Full Moon Phase Efforts" in part 2.

Wort Moon Party Ideas

★ Decorate with the colors and items suggested in the preceding "Circle Ideas" section.

★ Have a potluck picnic, with everyone contributing an entrée. Provide herbal iced tea with mint sprigs, rolls, herbed butter, and herbal cookies.

★ Make herbal sachets with everyone contributing an herb from the garden or kitchen cabinet. Provide tulle netting and ribbons, then have guests mix blends suitable to their personal magical purposes.

★ This is also a good time to make herbal incenses. Charge the herbs for specific magical purposes, mix in the blender with sawdust, and store in jars or zippered bags. Burn on charcoal blocks.

★ Have an herbal vinegar or wine-making[5] party. Ask everyone to contribute something, and make sure that all attendees receive a bottle of the finished product.

---

5. Simple instructions for making herbal wines and vinegars can be found in my book *Bud, Blossom & Leaf.* If you don't have a copy, search the Internet or your local library for instructions.

★ Make head wreaths from dried herbs and flowers using floral wire and ribbons. Give a small prize for the best wreath.

★ Ribbon-tied sprigs of herbs make great party favors.

AUGUST: THE BARLEY MOON

Thematic Energy

Since the Barley Moon heralds the beginning of the grain harvest, it holds a very special significance to the Witch. Why? Because grain holds all the mysteries of the life cycles in its very core. Each kernel, a product of the first grain ever grown, sprouts verdantly from the Earth. Each individual sprout grows tall and lush. And though each stalk dies at harvest, every seed that falls from death sprouts anew in the moist, fertile womb of the Mother.

This not only provides a perfect illustration of how the mysteries of birth, death, and rebirth cycle through Nature, but keeps us ever mindful that we are the grain of the human species. Because we all stem from the very first pair of human beings, we are all connected to each other, so these life cycles and mysteries not only belong to us, they are our heritage; for we, as the grain, provide the link to eternal life.

Magical Efforts

Because the energy of the Barley Moon brings eternal connectivity to the forefront, it provides an excellent time to work on issues that involve immediate or extended family, and matters that involve personal rebirths and endings. It's also an ideal time to mend relationships. Efforts involving new partnerships or relationships, both business and personal, come to fruition easily now too, as do legal matters that revolve around wills, legacies, and inheritances. This is also a good time to give thanks. Start with the Ancients, but don't forget the ancestors whose blood runs through your veins. Remember that it's only because of their existence that you live, breathe, and perpetuate the cycles of eternal life.

Sample Barley Moon Invocation

> *O Mother of All, O Queen of Connection*
> *I ask to become a perfect reflection*
> *Of Your warmth and Your beauty, Your nurturing love*
> *As You course through my Spirit, keep me mindful of*
> *Those who came before me—whose blood in my veins*
> *Has molded and shaped me—whose traits I retain*
> *And form me to be who You now envision*
> *A connection devised of Your perfect precision*

Barley Moon Circle Ideas

★ Wear shades of yellow, gold, and tan to symbolize the grain harvest.

★ Cover the altar with a yellow cloth, and decorate with ancestor photos and mementoes, ears of corn, bundles of wheat, and sheaves of grain.

★ Use yellow-gold candles and burn patchouli as incense. Alternatively, use Full Moon Incense. (For the recipe, see "Full Moon Phase Efforts" in part 2.)

★ Asperge the Circle with a small bundle of wheat or milo maize. After ritual, leave it and any grains used as altar decorations outdoors for the birds.

★ Outline the Circle area with paper chains to symbolize eternal life.

★ Serve oatmeal cookies and beer, or a nonalcoholic malt beverage.

★ For spell work appropriate to this Moon, see "Full Moon Phase Efforts" in part 2.

Barley Moon Party Ideas

★ Decorate with the colors and items suggested in the preceding "Circle Ideas" section.

★ Serve oatmeal cookies, wheat crackers with spreadable cheese, or whole grain rolls with butter, and beer or nonalcoholic malt beverages.

★ Hold an ancestor circle. Just ask everyone to bring a picture (or a memento) of a favorite ancestor. Allow your guests to tell stories about their ancestors, and how those people unwittingly changed their lives.

★ Play relay games to symbolize connectivity. Since the weather is warm, outdoor races are a good bet. If indoor games are more your style, try connect-the-dot pictures for children and a continuing story game for adults, with everyone taking a turn.

★ Since connectivity is about togetherness as well as bloodlines, make plans to do something as a team.

Visit a hospital ward for the terminally ill, deliver a meal to the homeless, or even adopt a section of a highway. The actual project you decide upon isn't important as long as you do it together and the results of the effort make a difference in someone's life.

★ Give braided bracelets of white, black, and red ribbons, symbolizing the cycle of life, death, and rebirth, as party favors.

SEPTEMBER: THE WINE OR HARVEST MOON

Thematic Energy

Commonly known as the Wine or Harvest Moon, this Moon arrives during the peak of the grape harvest. Wine was important to ancient cultures since it altered the condition of conscious awareness—often to the point that partakers of the substance seemed to float off into a trancelike state—and because of this, they believed that it opened the door to the wisdom and knowledge of the Divine. Therefore, the Wine Moon festival is a celebration of the Higher Self and its power.

Magical Efforts

The energies connected with this Moon provide a perfect time to still the body and let the Spirit take over. For this reason, efforts that involve meditation, divination, scrying, psychic development, or astral travel are good bets. Projects that involve guidance, answers, solutions, or truth discovery also work well now.

Sample Wine/Harvest Moon Invocation

> *O Mother Goddess, now hear my plea*
> *And open the world of the Spirit to me*
> *Open my eyes as You fling forth the door*
> *That I may see clearly what You have in store*
> *Open my ears that I hear with no doubt*
> *Open my mind to the Higher Self's route*
> *And open my heart, Lady—this most of all—*
> *Make me Your vessel, O Mother of All*

Wine/Harvest Moon Circle Ideas

★ Wear shades of purple, lavender, and puce to honor the grape harvest and the wisdom of the Divine Self.

★ Cover the altar with a purple cloth, and decorate with bunches of grapes and tiny grapevine wreaths.

★ Use purple or lavender candles and burn a mixture of allspice, mugwort, and sage as incense. Alternatively, use Full Moon Incense. (For the recipe, see "Full Moon Phase Efforts" in part 2.)

★ Cast the Circle with the wand or a piece of grapevine tied with purple ribbons to which bells have been attached. Ring the bells frequently during the casting and the ritual to awaken the Divine Self.

★ Serve peanut butter and/or grape jelly on graham crackers, and wine or grape juice for libation.

★ For spell work appropriate to this Moon, see "Full Moon Phase Efforts" in part 2.

Wine/Harvest Moon Party Ideas

★ Decorate with the colors and items suggested in the preceding "Circle Ideas" section.

★ Serve wine and cheese with grapes and other fruits of the season. Alternative menus might include grape juice accompanying pimento cheese sandwiches or cheddar cheese soup served with French bread.

★ Tease the spiritual brain by playing intuitive games. For example, you might ask each person to think of a simple object and have the others guess what it is. Another idea is to have one person start a sentence and see if the next person can finish the thought. Keep it simple and let everyone have a turn.

★ Have attendees bring their favorite divination tools. Ask them to give short demos of how the tools work and share tips they've picked up along the way. An exchange of mini-readings can also be fun, provided they're kept to a five-minute maximum and everyone gets a turn.

★ Toast the grape harvest gods with wine or grape juice. A sample toast might go something like this:

> *To Dionysus—Bacchus, too*
> *In Wine and Harvest, these gods rule*
> *But most of all, I toast to you*
> *That Wisdom guides you straight and true*

Be sure to save some of the liquid to pour on the ground as libation.

★ Give small packets of Spirit incense (a powdered mixture of bay leaves, nutmeg, and sage) tied in purple ribbons as party favors.

OCTOBER: THE BLOOD MOON

Thematic Energy

Receiving Her name from the opening of Fall hunting seasons, the significance of the Blood Moon's celebration is two-fold: it keeps us mindful of the importance of the life/death/rebirth cycles and honors those animals who gave their lives that we might survive. While many people shun hunting today, it was necessary in ancient times to feed the masses. More important than that, the hunt was considered a sacred rite. The hunter not only took sole responsibility for the life of the animal harvested (a responsibility that included assistance in the crossing-over process), but in using each portion of the animal in some way, gave it the gift of immortality.

For this reason, the celebration of the Blood Moon is one of honor and thanksgiving. Animals aren't the only ones honored, though. We also give thanks to the fruits, grains, and vegetables that died so we might live. Give some thought to immortalizing these wonderful creatures by using their byproducts—seeds, peels, shells, small bones, and so on—in your magic.

Magical Efforts

Because this Moon commemorates the cycles of life, death, and rebirth, nearly any magical effort works well now. However, it's an especially good time for work that deals with breaking bad habits, separations, goals that require decrease, health issues that require the removal of disease, and the close of any life chapter to bring about a new beginning.

Sample Blood Moon Invocation

O Mother, we now give You thanks
For creatures who grow on Your banks
Who live in forests, fields, and sea
Who give their very lives that we
May exist from day to day
And on this note it's that we pray
You keep us mindful of the toll
That life has placed upon their role

Blood Moon Circle Ideas

★ Wear shades of red, wine, and scarlet to honor those who gave their lives that you might live.

★ Cover the altar with a red or burgundy cloth, and adorn with Indian corn, apples, pumpkins, and pictures of animals.

★ Use red candles and burn a mixture of cinnamon, nutmeg, and ginger as incense. Alternatively, use Full Moon Incense. (For the recipe, see "Full Moon Phase Efforts" in part 2.)

★ Cast the circle with an antler or an ear of Indian corn tied in red ribbons.

★ Invite pets into Circle, and give them special treats as a token of your gratitude for the many ways they enrich your life. Allow some time to play with them in Circle as well.

★ Serve red wine and gingersnaps for libation. For a nonalcoholic alternative, serve apple cider to which a little red food coloring has been added.

★ For spell work appropriate to this Moon, see "Full Moon Phase Efforts" in part 2.

Blood Moon Party Ideas

★ Decorate with the colors and items suggested in the preceding "Circle Ideas" section.

★ Serve chili, beef stew, or tomato soup with hot bread and butter.

★ Before sitting down to eat, light a red candle and give personal thanks to those who gave their life for yours. Pass the candle to the next person and have them do the same. When everyone has spoken, place the candle in the center of the table and let it burn throughout the meal.

★ Ask all attendees to bring a donation for the local animal shelter (this could include blankets, towels, food, toys, and so forth), then make the delivery together. Spend some time playing with the animals, then sign up to volunteer a few hours of your time this month.

★ This particular Moon provides an excellent time to play hunting games of all sorts. Hide something in the house, divide your guests into teams, then provide them with a set of clues. Give a small prize to the first team that finds the object.

★ Give each attendee an apple, a pomegranate, and a small white candle to take home. Instruct the attendees to light the candle to guide the dead to the Summerland, and to leave the fruit outside to feed them on the journey.

★ Recipes from your personal collection make great party favors. (Take care in choosing who gets which recipe, though. It wouldn't do for a vegetarian to wind up with your favorite recipe for beef stroganoff!)

NOVEMBER: THE SNOW MOON

Thematic Energy

The fullness of the Snow Moon heralds the dark months of the year. It also signals Mother Earth that it's time to get some well-deserved rest. Exhausted from the constant activity of planting, growing, and harvesting, She yawns and stretches, and settles in for a long winter's nap. As the snows fall to cover Her with an insulating blanket, all of Nature follows suit. Plants and trees recede into dormancy, and animals retreat to nests and dens. In fact, it's almost as if they know the Earth has gone to bed, and take the opportunity to rest as well.

But Mother Earth and Nature aren't the only ones resting. So are we. With fewer hours of sunlight and the coming of the cooler weather, we find ourselves spending more time indoors. We tie up loose ends, finish projects, and find time to relax and regenerate. We also contemplate the goodness of the Earth, the wonder of friends and family, and all that makes our lives worth living. We take time to count our blessings, and they are many.

Magical Efforts

While the coming of the Snow Moon brings a great time for dreamwork, it also lends its energies easily to meditational efforts, divinatory efforts, and projects that require endings. Use it also for setting magical goals into motion, as well as planning for the reinvention of your life.

Sample Snow Moon Invocation

> *We call You forth, Mother, for a last goodnight kiss*
> *Before You drift off to slumber and rest in its bliss*
> *We ask that You help us to tie up loose ends*
> *To complete all the projects that we must now tend*
> *So that we, too, can rest when our work is all done*
> *And recharge and regroup for that which will come*
> *And as You rest peacefully, this thing please know:*
> *We are thankful for all that You bring and bestow*

Snow Moon Circle Ideas

★ Dress in dark colors—black, navy blue, and purple are all good choices—to commemorate the sleeping of the Earth.

★ Cover the altar with a sheet or a quilt, and decorate with potatoes, onions, garlic, turnips, and other vegetables that grow beneath the ground.

★ Use purple or dark blue candles and burn mugwort or patchouli as incense. Alternatively, use Full Moon Incense. (For the recipe, see "Full Moon Phase Efforts" in part 2.)

★ Asperge the Circle with water to which you've added a bit of camphor. If that's not possible, dissolve a little Mentholatum in hot water for use as a substitution.

★ Serve herbed wine and sugar cookies for libation. Serve milk as a nonalcoholic alternative.

★ Close the Circle by singing a lullaby to the Earth. Use the winning lullaby from the contest you held at the Storm Moon, or try something to the tune of "Brahms' Lullaby" like:

> *Mother Earth, get some rest*
> *Peaceful dreams while You're sleeping*
> *Gain new strength, for the Spring-time's*
> *Work will shortly come*

★ For spell work appropriate to this Moon, see "Full Moon Phase Efforts" in part 2.

Snow Moon Party Ideas

★ Decorate with the colors suggested in the preceding "Circle Ideas" section. For a centerpiece, fashion a bed from a shoebox, and add a small pillow and blanket, then place a mini-globe of the world inside and pull up the covers.

★ Serve French onion soup, or potato soup topped with grilled onions and garlic. If this is a "drink only" party, serve hot buttered rum or hot spiced cider.

★ Write a poem of thanksgiving to the Mother Earth, with each person contributing a line, then pay homage by reciting it together aloud.

★ Have a dream analyzing session, with each attendee sharing a dream and the rest of the group working to shed light on its meaning.

★ Ask each attendee to bring two four-inch squares of cloth and small quantities of dream herbs (good choices are chamomile, mugwort, rosemary, lavender, poppy seed, and rose petals). Provide needles, thread, and polyester fiberfill so everyone can make a dream pillow. (For detailed instructions, see "Full Moon Phase Efforts" in part 2.)

★ Give glow-in-the-dark stars and moons as party favors.

5

The Celestial Connection

While the energies of specific Moon phases can be very
important when it comes to magical, mundane, or even
gardening results, there's something else that can make
or break our success rates. It's a valuable tool. A wonderful tool. A tool so magically powerful that it can send
even the most shoddily constructed spell soaring right
into the Universe. Simply put, it's the astrological sign
through which the Moon travels.

Sadly enough, we seldom put this tool to use. Why?
There are many reasons. Some folks don't think it really
matters, arguing that a strong intent is all that's necessary for effective magic. Others feel that waiting until the
Moon cycles through a particular sign takes too long.
But the most common reason that folks don't use this
tool is because they simply forget it's there. And when it
comes to magic, that's very sad, indeed.

The fact of the matter is that magic *can* manifest
whether you work in harmony with the Moon's astrological sign or not. And yes, magic *is* geared to make your
life easier instead of more difficult. But refusing to use a

tool that will give your magic an edge it wouldn't normally have? Well, let's just say that it's the most ridiculous thing I've ever heard.

If you were preparing a garden and had the option of using a tiller as opposed to a hoe, there wouldn't be any question as to choice. The same is true of using a dishwasher versus washing dishes by hand, or reading by electric lighting as opposed to a candle flame. And yet, when it comes to magic—something that should be as second nature to practitioners as flipping the proverbial light switch—folks find countless reasons for complete and utter dismissal. Dismissal despite the fact that including this tool in every effort can do more to bring magical manifestation than all the wand-waving in the world. It's just like throwing the baby out with the bathwater; it's not only silly, it's absolutely absurd.

That's all well and fine. But what does the Moon's astrological sign have to do with magic? Or more to the point, how can it boost magical manifestation and bring more exacting results?

Just as the Moon's phases exude different energies, so does Her astrological sign. This means that the Moon's energies are more effective for certain efforts when She's traveling through a sign that's in harmony with the work at hand. To give you an idea of how this tool leaves its imprint on virtually everything in our lives, let's look at how it can affect something as common to human nature as an intimate relationship. In fact, let's take a look at how various Moon signs figured in to the steps that led to my marriage.

The Moon was in Taurus when I first laid eyes on my husband. And there wasn't a doubt in my mind that he was "the one." Had I met him during another astrological phase, though, that might not have been the case. Why? Because Taurus Moon energies not only add spice to romance, but vibrate toward stability and long-term plans. The Moon's energy was so strong that day that it couldn't help but affect us, or the lasting relationship that was to follow.

Our first date came when the Moon was in Leo, and we couldn't have picked a better time. That's because the Leo Moon is a great time to start new relationships. It vibrates toward social interaction and the need to put your best foot forward. Best of all, though, it brings forth the urge to have fun. And we all know that a first date without fun seldom makes for a second!

We moved in together during a Cancer Moon (a time to set goals and tend to affairs of the home and hearth), and the proposal came when the Moon was in Libra (a time of romance, self-awareness, and balance). The Moon, however, was cycling through Virgo on our wedding day. And while many folks wouldn't see this as a good time to seal a relationship (though romantic, Virgo also brings lots of structure) such was not the case for us. Why? Because even though our lifestyle isn't what most people might consider traditional, we both thrive on structured, service-oriented, old-fashioned values, and that's exactly what Virgo brings to our marriage.

The point is this: Even though we didn't plan our relationship around various Moon signs, there's no doubt that their energies affected the outcome. If they can bring that much to the lives of two perfect strangers, just imagine what they can add to your magic! That being the case, be a smart practitioner. Take advantage of this wonderful tool both magically and mundanely. Your efforts will reap the benefits, and so will you.

For your convenience the following charts are divided into three sections: Magical Work, Mundane Event Planning, and Gardening Tips. Please understand that this chart is designed as a starting point only, and is not the "have all and be all" of astrological Moon planning. Don't hesitate to stray from or add to the efforts listed below. After working with the different Moon signs, you may discover that their energies affect you differently. You may even hit upon something so magically fabulous that it sends your efforts soaring into the Universe like nothing you've ever encountered. And to miss out on that just because you were afraid to venture forth would spell travesty, indeed!

MOON IN ARIES

Magical Work

The Aries Moon vibrates toward courage, leadership, victory, awards, and challenges of every sort. It's effective for workings involving soldiers and war, competitions and battles, and health issues. And because its energies definitely set the stage for getting things done, it also provides the perfect time for working on short-term goals. Use it, too, for blessing and consecrating the athame and censor.

Mundane Event Planning

Since the energy of this Moon lends itself to resolution and tying up loose ends, there's no better time for preventative maintenance. Such maintenance could include anything from scheduling your yearly physical, oil changes and tune-ups for your vehicle, or replacing the weather stripping and central air filters in your home. It also provides a good time to apply for jobs and send resumes, collect debts, and enter contests.

Gardening Tips

Because Aries is a Fire sign, it's classified as "barren." While you won't want to plant anything just now, it is an excellent time to weed, cultivate the soil, and prune to deter growth. This is also a good time to harvest any herbs you wish to dry.

MOON IN TAURUS

Magical Work

When this Moon comes to call, work on efforts that require long-lasting results. Good candidates for this energy include home affairs and matters of finance, as well as efforts that involve stability, security, and protection. It's also useful for resolving issues related to self-esteem, and for adding spice and romance to intimate relationships.

Mundane Event Planning

Taurus Moon energy is stable, sensuous, and luxurious, and lends itself to all matters that make us feel secure, pampered, and worthwhile. For this reason, its appearance not only provides a good time to buy a new home (or delve into remodeling or redecorating the one you already have), but to open bank accounts, reorganize stock portfolios, and restructure retirement plans. Don't discount it either when it comes to meeting the perfect mate, for love affairs begun during this Moon tend to be constant, stable, and long-lasting.

Gardening Tips

Any root crops (carrots, potatoes, radishes, and so on) planted now tend to bring a very fruitful harvest. This is also a good time to fertilize.

MOON IN GEMINI

Magical Work

Since Gemini is the sign of communication, this Moon provides the perfect energies for anything requiring inspiration and inventiveness. Use its power to retain knowledge, write spells and rituals, or work on efforts involving business ventures or matters that require a quick resolution. This Moon sign also provides an excellent time for blessing and consecrating wands, and performing protection rituals regarding automobiles.

Mundane Event Planning

While this Moon definitely brings the right energy for writing articles, giving speeches, and starting new projects, no other energy compares when it comes to having your ideas well-received by business associates or authority figures. Use the Gemini Moon for obtaining and signing contracts, presenting proposals, or voicing new ideas, as well as for planning trips and handling related details. Its energy also lends itself toward the purchase or update of phone equipment, computers, and peripherals.

Gardening Tips

The Gemini Moon brings a good time to harvest herb and root crops. Flowers cut now stay fresher longer. This is also the best time to dry them for future use.

MOON IN CANCER

Magical Work

The only sign ruled by the Moon, Cancer energy lends itself to emotional issues, inner journeys, and psychic development, as well as efforts that require goal-setting, personal growth, self-empowerment, nurturement, compassion, and forgiveness. It's also powerful when used in efforts that involve weather-working, or the home and hearth, especially when it comes to blessings related to food, personal space, or the consecration of your altar.

Mundane Event Planning

Because of its connection to both the psychic and emotional realms, the Cancer Moon brings several possibilities for event planning. Magically speaking, it provides an excellent time to embark on new courses of divinatory or metaphysical study. From a more mundane standpoint, though, its energies are invaluable when it comes to matters of the home, whether it be the search for new living quarters or just a simplification of affairs and personal belongings in the current one. It also provides a good time for proposals of marriage or long-term commitment, as well as wedding and handfasting ceremonies.

Gardening Tips

Plant all leafy crops now, especially those that bear fruit. This is also a good time to encourage growth by cutting back.

MOON IN LEO

Magical Work

When the Moon travels through Leo, it provides the perfect energy for efforts that involve friendship, the forming of new relationships, and a complete reinvention of life as you know it. It also harmonizes well with magical endeavors that relate to self-expression or the development of personal talents.

Mundane Event Planning

Want to throw a successful party? Schedule it for a time when the Moon is in Leo! There's no other Moon energy that lends itself so fully to showmanship, social interaction, or fun. And since self-devotion is also a part of this Moon's package, take care to schedule vacations for this period, too. They'll not only be rewarding, but packed with long-lasting memories.

Gardening Tips

Since Leo is the most barren of the signs, save all planting for another time. This energy is very useful, however, for tilling the soil and the complete eradication of weeds and garden pests.

MOON IN VIRGO

Magical Work

Because the energy of the Virgo Moon lends itself to anything that requires detailed organization, use it to boost matters involving finance, structure, productivity, and the completion of old projects. It also lends itself to romantic endeavors where traditional values are important.

Mundane Event Planning

Since organization is key when the Virgo Moon appears, use it to clear away clutter and discard the old and useless; this includes not only material possessions, but worn-out ideas. Then devise new systems for handling everything in life more efficiently. This is also a good time to schedule surgeries, both major and minor. Other good bets for this energy might include the signing of contracts, financial planning, service-oriented efforts like volunteer work, and future plans that involve a committed relationship.

Gardening Tips

Another barren sign, this energy is best used to make initial garden and soil preparations, and handle weed and pest problems.

MOON IN LIBRA

Magical Work

When the Moon swings into Libra, balance comes to the forefront. For this reason, it works well in efforts that require justice, compromise, cooperation, and teamwork. Because of its Venusian nature, it also lends itself to endeavors that involve romance, beauty, and self-awareness.

Mundane Event Planning

Because of the equalizing energies of Libra Moon, this is a good time to work with all matters that require balance or a sense of fair play. This could include everything from bank statements to wills to court appearances. Since this sign is ruled by Venus, it also provides the perfect energy for romance and beauty, so use it for buying a new wardrobe, updating your hairstyle, or creating a whole new you. Don't discount it for first dates, initiating long-term intimate relationships, making love with a new partner, and wedding or handfasting ceremonies.

Gardening Tips

Even though Libra is at the bottom of the list when it comes to fruitful signs, it's very beneficial when it comes to planting flowers, ground cover, or vines.

MOON IN SCORPIO

Magical Work

The Scorpio Moon has a raw, pure energy that makes it perfect for efforts involving sex magic. It also lends itself to magical work involving psychism, separation, truth, transformational change, courage, wishes, and goal accomplishment. Use it also for blessing and consecrating scrying mirrors, crystal balls, or other divinatory tools.

Mundane Event Planning

When drastic measures are necessary for personal growth (setting plans in motion for long-range goals comes to mind here), nothing can beat the transformational and separating energies of the Scorpio Moon. For this reason, save any life-altering decision-making such as cross-country moves, career changes, relationship endings, and so forth for this time. It's also useful for surgical procedures where growth, tumor, or cyst removal are at issue, as well as the commencement of treatment for other health problems. But those aren't the only things this energy is good for. It's also great for buying new bed linens and lingerie, and using them to their full advantage!

Gardening Tips

A very fruitful sign, seeds sown during a Scorpio Moon tend to germinate very quickly. It's also a good time to prune if you want to encourage the growth of leaf or flower buds.

MOON IN SAGITTARIUS

Magical Work

Because this Moon sign is the most inquisitive in nature, it can be a great help when it comes to magical efforts that require data retrieval or the attainment of long overdue answers. Its energies also pack a wallop when it comes to any work involving control issues, optimism, self-confidence, and friendship, and can be a real boost to those that relate to legal matters, good luck, and prophetic dreaming.

Mundane Event Planning

If you've thought about going back to school, now is the time to do it; knowledge gleaned from classes taken during this Moon sign will stick with you forever. Since solutions and answers come easily now as well, work on projects that require research or problems that require tact and diplomacy. This Moon isn't all about work, though—it's also about spontaneity, so it's great for taking a vacation, throwing an impromptu party, getting together with friends, or forming new relationships.

Gardening Tips

Another barren sign, the Sagittarius Moon is best used for soil cultivation and harvesting. Since its energies also discourage growth, it's a good time to cut plants back before putting the garden to bed.

MOON IN CAPRICORN

Magical Work

If you have problems with self-control, personal discipline, or if you lack structure in your life, the Capricorn Moon can help you to set things right. This energy is also beneficial to magical efforts that involve career, focus, self-confidence, and personal goals and ambitions—especially those where some sort of sacrifice is necessary—as well as those that require logic, strategy, and a certain amount of practicality. It's also a good time to bless and consecrate the altar pentacle.

Mundane Event Planning

Since Capricorn's energy smacks of structure, anything that requires building or construction (this could include work projects, team efforts, reconstructive surgeries, a restructuring of the family unit, reorganizing your life, or home building projects) is a good bet at this time. And while this Moon provides an excellent time to apply for credit, reorganize investments, and build balances in your bank accounts, it's also perfect for starting that diet or personal exercise program.

Gardening Tips

A fruitful Earth sign, the Capricorn Moon provides a good time to plant rhizome, bulb, or stalk crops. (Mints, irises, tulips, celery, and rhubarb all come to mind here.) Any branches pruned now will grow back much stronger than they were initially.

MOON IN AQUARIUS

Magical Work

Although the Aquarian energies are flexible in nature—and this opens a wealth of possibility for magical work—they truly focus on the self. For this reason, efforts involving creativity, individuality, independence, and optimism work well now, as well as those that deal with humanitarianism, friendships, and personal interaction in group dynamics.

Mundane Event Planning

Since the Aquarius Moon brings the personal to light, this is a good time to pamper yourself. Make plans for a manicure, pedicure, hair cut, and massage, or maybe even spend a whole day at the spa. It's also a good time to contemplate and explore your options. This might include reading the fine print in contracts, checking the details of an impending move, throwing yourself into some investigative research regarding a career change, or refinancing your home. This is truly a time for looking at how things affect you and for tending to your best interests, so an inner journey may be necessary before plunging into anything new.

Gardening Tips
Literally any crop—leaf, stalk, flower, or root—may be successfully harvested now. It's also a good time to work with soil cultivation.

MOON IN PISCES

Magical Work
The sensitivity of the Pisces Moon delves deep into the core of the inner self. For this reason, its energies are excellent to use for projects that involve imagination, inspiration, and artistic skill, as well as those that involve intuition, psychic development, meditation, or past lives. Because this energy also brings swift personal balance between the mundane and spiritual worlds, it also provides a good time to bless and consecrate the cup.

Mundane Event Planning
The Pisces Moon provides an excellent time to settle disputes of a sensitive nature, whether they be between friends or family. It's also helpful when it comes to resolving those nasty inner struggles that we seem to have with ourselves from time to time. Plans for creative endeavors—this includes everything from writing proposals and

contracts to drawing up blueprints for a house—also
benefit greatly from the wondrous energy of this Moon.
But that's not all. Use this energy for cleaning out closets, getting rid of the old and useless, and making way
for the new and wonderful.

Gardening Tips

Any crops planted under this Moon enjoy the luxury of
strong, well-formed root systems. For this reason, it's also
an excellent time to transplant.

WHICH WITCH IS WHICH?

We already know that certain efforts bring better results
when performed as the Moon cycles through a particular phase or astrological sign, but there's something else
that can boost results as well. This incredible tool pulses
with energy and writhes with power, then it waits patiently
in hopes that we'll notice its existence and put it to good
use. Unfortunately, most of us don't. And that's really
sad, because for the most part it's what truly sets us apart
as individuals. Simply put, this tool is the personal Moon
sign.

What does this have to do with magic? Everything! To
a large degree, the personal Moon sign decrees how we
act and react to any given situation. It not only governs
the way we handle our problems, but often determines
how far we'll go to justify our solutions. More importantly, though, it holds dominion over our innermost
feelings, and emotion—raw, uncut, and pure—is the

matrix from which all magic flows. It only stands to reason that a magical effort performed when the Moon cycles through the personal sign can enjoy a boost of power that others cannot.

But that's not the only reason that the personal Moon sign is of major importance. Knowing and understanding this sign brings magical specialties into view, and even though there really aren't any limits when it comes to magic, such an understanding can also provide knowledge into areas you may want to leave alone.

Take me, for example. Being one of the major occult signs, my Scorpio Moon provides a wealth of magical ability. I tend to do very well with divinatory efforts. Spellcasting comes so easily to me that I've seldom had a spell fall flat. In fact, my spells usually work *too* well, and believe it or not, that's also where my downfall exists.

You see, the Scorpio Moon makes me an incredibly emotional practitioner, which is one of the reasons that my magic works so well. Unfortunately, it also brings me the ability to hide that emotion so deeply from others that at times even I don't realize it exists. Not knowing how much emotion there already is, I tend to build it until it is absolutely bursting. And while my magical efforts are definitely successful, they often bring long-lasting after-effects and take far too much of my energy. It's a little like using a hammer to swat a fly.

With a Scorpio Moon, I also have to be extremely careful of anger. This sign not only refuses to forget, it is the sneakiest in the group. In fact, it will happily spend twenty years or more just to get the perfect revenge. This sort of attitude not only has no place in magic, but left unchecked, tends to bite the practitioner in the butt. Therefore, I not only have to be careful of my thoughts and spend extra time grounding myself, I must constantly weigh my feelings with my intent in order to come up with an appropriate solution.

What if you don't know the sign of your personal Moon? What then? Just gather your birth information (date, time, and location) and have your natal chart run. Failing that, plug the information into one of the great astrological software programs available in stores everywhere and do it yourself. Either way, the information will come up and you'll be well on your way.

Once you know your Moon sign, check the appropriate section in the pages that follow. Though brief, the information listed is designed to bring insight into your magical strong points and weaknesses, and provide daily affirmations for squelching the personal problem areas. More importantly, it will help you to understand yourself, and that's the best tool you can have when practicing magic.

ARIES MOON SIGN

Aries Moon practitioners seldom dwell upon their problems. Why? Because these folks understand that time and energy are valuable commodities, and know that applying either to a negative situation only serves to feed the negativity. They take action—swift, expedient action—

that removes the problem at its source and casts it from their lives. This full-steam-ahead attitude makes them excellent candidates for magical efforts that involve motivation, efficiency, and productivity, as well as those that require a battle of sorts.

Unfortunately, this innate need to act is also to the practitioner's detriment. You see, Aries often acts first and thinks later. It seldom looks at what caused a chain of events. Instead, it only sees the outcome. It only knows what it feels. Assuming an injustice, it runs off, headstrong and half-cocked, to rectify things. Of course, this sort of attitude not only causes serious problems when it comes to magical work, but can bring swift and unexpected Karmic retribution.

Aries Moon Affirmation

> *I am the magic where action is key*
> *But before acting, I look carefully*
> *At the course of events that lead up to the end*
> *And I think long and hard about what I should spend*
> *On rectification, or whether it's best*
> *To pass them along unto Karma's true test*

TAURUS MOON SIGN

Those born under the Taurus Moon are perhaps the most patient of all magical practitioners. They simply don't expect things to work right away. And why not? Because they know that anything worthwhile is worth waiting for, and they understand that perfection—something that's really important to them—doesn't just happen overnight. In fact, they often see magical operations as a construction process, much like putting together a comfortable home. Such things take careful planning, tasteful positioning, and painstaking application before they can manifest. For these reasons, the magical expertise of Taurus Moon practitioners lies in efforts involving long-range goals and accomplishments, the building of relationships and partnerships, and those things that require a good amount of patience and somewhat tedious handling.

Just like the other moon signs, though, Taurus has its drawbacks. For one thing, there is nothing more stubborn than these practitioners, especially once they've decided upon a particular magical method. Want them to change their minds? Maybe see things your way? Good luck! It's just not going to happen, not even if they're wrong. Couple that with the fact that they overdo everything—they truly do think that more is better—and it can be a magical fiasco in the making.

Taurus Moon Affirmation

> *I am the most patient of all the magicians*
> *I plan and I plod putting all in position*
> *I'm as solid as Earth, but must learn to accept*
> *That change equals growth and it's part of the set*
> *Of laws that rule living and magic and more*
> *And that stubbornness locks opportunity's door*

GEMINI MOON SIGN

Because Gemini is ruled by Mercury, those born under this Moon sign truly know how to communicate, and proper communication is especially important when it comes to magical work. They understand that the Universe is simply a vehicle fueled by proper instruction, and since they definitely know how to instruct, working magic within its confines just comes naturally. They're extremely specific in their requests. They never forget to dot their i's or cross their t's. In fact, with these practitioners, nothing is ever left to chance. That being the case, nearly any effort they perform not only manifests with the expected results, but manifests in record time. This means that difficult tasks, even those that seem next to impossible, benefit from the communicative expertise of Gemini Moon practitioners.

Just as the Air Element brings good communication skills, it can also bring a scattered sort of energy that results in air-headedness and a short attention span. And when these characteristics come into play, these practitioners can be very short-sighted. Their minds ricochet from one thing to another, causing them to start new projects before old ones are finished. Focus becomes a thing of the past. And how could it be otherwise? With their energies literally bouncing off the Cosmic wall, it's all they can do to put one foot in front of the other. The last thing on their minds is concentration, especially the sort it takes for successful magic.

Gemini Moon Affirmation

> *I hold the magical key to the word*
> *Whether verbal or written, unseen or unheard*
> *My thoughts are well-focused; they come across well—*
> *Neither scattered or tethered, but clear as a bell*
> *And as focus shifts toward this pure clarity*
> *I manifest all as I will it to be*

CANCER MOON SIGN

Love, nurturement, and compassion are key words of the Cancer Moon sign. These folks don't understand the meaning of the word "selfish." They're just not built that way. Ruled by intuition, they always seem to know what you need (even before you do) and will go to great lengths to make it happen. They're also more akin to home and hearth than any other sign under the Moon, and since most magical efforts are actually performed at home, this is good stuff. But the Cancer practitioner takes this one step further by effortlessly creating sacred space—an awe-inspiring sort of space that's not only comfortable and functional, but theirs alone—a perfect space where magic can grow and flourish. These qualities make them excellent candidates for all efforts involving home matters, gardening, love, and healing, as well as those that require an inordinate amount of intuitive power or psychism.

To their detriment, though, Cancer Moon sign practitioners have huge issues with emotional security; they simply don't trust well. And while it's one thing to not trust someone with their hearts or innermost secrets, this lack of faith can spell big trouble when it comes to magic. Why? Because not trusting the Universe to deliver results when performing an effort defeats the purpose. It's nothing less than magical sabotage, and that's a place that no practitioner wants to go.

Cancer Moon Affirmation

> *I am the magic that creates the space*
> *Where the manifestation of magic takes place*
> *And though it is comfortable there in that spot*
> *I learn to place trust in the realms that are not*
> *Perfect or flawless or certain or sure*
> *For that is where magic flows true, straight and pure*

LEO MOON SIGN

The Leo Moon is very powerful indeed when it comes to magical workings. Why? Because folks born under a Leo Moon never second-guess themselves. They know what they want. They know what they're doing. Most importantly, though, they know that every effort they perform will meet with success. Leo Moon practitioners do very well with magical efforts involving self-confidence, self-esteem, and self-worth, as well as those that call for a restructuring of personal characteristics.

So, what's the problem? Unfortunately, the Leo Moon tends to be full of itself. It often possesses a personal arrogance seldom found in other signs. Left unchecked, it can result in a know-it-all attitude, a lack of respect for the Universal Plan, and of course, the skipping of important magical steps. As far as the latter, anything even remotely inconvenient qualifies here, for those born under the Leo Moon can't be bothered with the slightest annoyance; it's beneath them and their stature. They tend to get frequent wake-up calls from the Universe— wake-up calls that knock them flat on their butts and leave them wondering what happened.

Leo Moon Affirmation

> *I am the Lion, and strong, though I am*
> *I adhere strictly to Life's Cosmic Plan*
> *Though I am the matrix from which magic flows*
> *I'm respectful of forces that make magic grow*
> *So I humble myself and I follow the way*
> *Of the natural path of all magic this day*

VIRGO MOON SIGN

The most organized of the Moon signs, Virgo has a real love of order, structure, and schematics. This is important magically, for those born under this Moon take the time to plan every step with such diligence that one flows flawlessly into the other. The result is a perfectly orchestrated effort; an effort that seldom, if ever, meets with anything but success. Virgo Moon practitioners shine when it comes to efforts that involve building, restructuring, removal, and complicated matters that require painstaking preparation.

The problem arises when things don't go according to plan. Because Virgo is the persnickety sort, it often forgets that magic doesn't always subscribe to the laws of logic. It fails to remember that creativity, rather than structure, is the basis for all change. So when things go awry, as they frequently do, Virgo Moon practitioners have trouble picking up the ball of improvisation. They simply sit there wishing that they had allowed for the problem instead of gathering the gumption to fly by the seat of their pants.

Virgo Moon Affirmation

> *A magical engineer, though I am*
> *I embrace changes that occur in my plans*
> *Regardless of structure, I twirl with the flow*
> *Applying the creative force as I go*
> *I check for all problems before they arise*
> *So magical efforts won't be jeopardized*

LIBRA MOON SIGN

Because Libra brings an equilibrium to magic that no other personal Moon sign can boast, practitioners born under this Moon float effortlessly between the realms of the spiritual and the mundane. They not only understand the theories of cause and effect and action and reaction, but understand why a system of magical checks and balances is necessary. Most importantly, though, they know how to put these magical components in place so all efforts flow through the Universe in flawless measure. For these reasons, Libra Moon practitioners do well in all efforts involving balance, fairness, good judgment, and justice.

As wonderful as that is, though, Libra often gets caught up in a magical juggling act of sorts. It's so concerned about perfect balance that it plays the "on-one-hand-this-on-the-other-hand-that" game until the world looks level. In fact, it often has difficulty making a firm decision about anything. As a result, nothing ever gets done. Magic simply sits on the shelf waiting, watching, and wondering whether it will ever take wing and fly.

Libra Moon Affirmation

> *I hold the scales of all balance in hand*
> *I weigh and I measure each magical plan*
> *And once calculated, then on I progress*
> *Without further thought, without second guess,*
> *I move, taking action, as forward I go*
> *Releasing the effort so magic can flow*

SCORPIO MOON SIGN

Commonly known as the "occult sign" of the zodiac, it's been said that Scorpio is the ultimate when it comes to the magical arena. Why? Because most practitioners born under this Moon not only have the ability to cut through the surface, find what's beneath, and use it to its best advantage, but can manage it all with little or no effort. Since magic depends on tapping into and controlling the power of the unseen, this is very important, indeed. Scorpio Moon practitioners excel at all magical efforts, but most find that their real specialty is divination.

Scorpio is also an extremely emotional sign. Although emotion is the catalyst for all magic, this level of emotion is often to the practitioner's detriment. The problem is that Scorpio is a sneaky sort. It not only hides its true feelings away from the world (which in itself is a dishonest thing to do), but buries them so deeply that even they can't find them. Not understanding that these emotions already exist, they build them to overflow for magical work. It's not only overkill, but can cause all sorts of Karmic backlash, especially when anger is involved.

Scorpio Moon Affirmation

> *I unearth the unseen and I bring it to light*
> *I uncover the hidden so magic takes flight*
> *But I do not bury my feelings inside*
> *I deal with them honestly so they can't hide*
> *Then I use their power to set my work free*
> *And fill my magic with pure energy*

SAGITTARIUS MOON SIGN

Sagittarius Moon practitioners are confident and optimistic. They are also natural leaders. You'll often find them relating personal anecdotes of how they managed success against all odds. No need to think that arrogance is a factor, though, for nothing could be further from the truth. These folks are quick to point out their own faulty decisions, and laugh about them, in the hope that those listening won't fall into the same traps. With an attitude of "If I can do it, so can you," they not only bring a sense of self-confidence where it's sorely lacking, but empower all around them with words of encouragement and well-needed pats on the back. For this reason, Sagittarius Moon practitioners excel when it comes to efforts involving independence, success, victory, and goal accomplishment, as well as those that require an inordinate amount of self-confidence.

These Moon practitioners also have a real desire for knowledge and always seem to be searching out the truth. And while that quality may seem admirable (at least at first glance), it can really wreak havoc when it comes to magic. Why? Because these folks not only want to know how magic works and why it works, but what makes it work like it does. They want to pick it apart, muss it up beyond all recognition, and then see if it will fit back together again. In fact, they get so caught up in the wonderment of it all that they often forget about two really important things: that magic works, plain and simple, regardless of how or why or what, and the original reason they wanted to perform a magical effort at all.

Sagittarius Moon Affirmation

Mine is the search for the truth of all things
What it is, why it works, how it flies without wings

And while that is a part of the magical key
I learn to accept that things work naturally
Without wherefores and whys—without reason or rule—
I am the most potent of magical tools

CAPRICORN MOON SIGN

Because Capricorn brings a common sense approach to life, those born under its Moon are the most pragmatic of practitioners. Structured and practical, they seldom waste time on nonsensical frills. They have a real knack for trimming things down to the bare bones, tend to use whatever they have on hand to get the job done, and understand that less is more. These folks make wonderful teachers and always see the big picture. This is great news when it comes to magical work, for not only do Capricorn Moon practitioners go into efforts understanding how their magic will affect others, they also see the need for a certain amount of mundane follow-through, which they incorporate into every effort. Because of this, they are excellent candidates for all efforts, but especially those that involve long-term goals or planning, or require an extra dose of strategy or logic.

As with all the other practitioners, though, these folks have their shortcomings. Because they're such practical planners—and so tied into logic, strategy, and personal responsibility—they tend to think that their way is the only way. Of course, this can cause all sorts of problems when it comes to their students, or even something as

simple as a discourse of magical ideas. One slight vari-
ance or disagreement, and the guilt trip comes out full
force. Not just any guilt trip, mind you, but the mother
of them all. They lay it on as thick as molasses, never
bothering to consider that if they'd only listen, they
might actually learn something that could make their
magic even more potent than it already is.

Capricorn Moon Affirmation

I am the teacher of magic profound
I hold the knowledge from whence it abounds
But I shake off the urge to make others conform
To my way of doing things as they perform
Their magical dance—and I learn as I go
Accepting suggestions without guilt trip or woe

AQUARIUS MOON SIGN

Aquarius brings an idealistic approach to life, and those
born under its Moon are the most imaginative of practitioners. Much preferring the realm of unconventionality
and nonconformity, they seldom waste time on anything
status quo. Instead, they march to their own drummers
while embracing a personal sense of independence—but
that doesn't mean that they don't know how to get things
done. Because the ruling Water Element gives them a
unique sort of flexibility, Aquarius Moon practitioners
not only recover quickly from last minute changes, but
can rise to meet any challenge. These qualities make
them excellent candidates for performing all efforts that

require imagination and inspiration, as well as change, transformation, and freedom.

The only problem with most folks born under the Aquarian Moon is that they seldom consider how any magic they perform (or anything else they do, for that matter) could affect the other people around them. Instead of looking at the big picture, they only worry about what might be to their personal benefit. Simply put—and I apologize in advance since there's just no polite way to phrase this—they tend to think that everything is about them. And when it comes to magical operations, nothing could be further from the truth. In fact, it's this very thing, the inflation of that wonderful Aquarian ego, that often brings results they neither expected nor prepared for.

Aquarius Moon Affirmation

> *I am the flow of the magical world*
> *With my inspiration, all magic's unfurled*
> *In my strategies, though, I must learn to allow*
> *For those that my magic affects here and now*
> *For the magical world is not just about me*
> *It reaches much further than my eyes can see*

PISCES MOON SIGN

Pisces is, perhaps, the most sensitive of all the personal Moon signs, and because of its association with the emotion of the Water Element, this sign can make for very powerful magic. It's also one of the most adaptable and discerning in the zodiac, and has the ability to roll with the flow and to determine when mundane action is more appropriate than that of a magical nature. This is important, because it's often the mundane steps that truly set magic into motion. That being the case, Pisces Moon practitioners excel at efforts involving flexibility and change, motivation and action, as well as those that require soothing raw emotions like jealousy, anger, and fear.

On the downside, hurt feelings, rather than anger, usually comprise the largest problem for practitioners with a Pisces Moon. Why? Because Pisces tends to stifle the hurt, and once pushed aside, it festers into other magical obstacles like loss of self-confidence, poor self-esteem, and various other insecurities. This, of course, tosses Pisces right into magical self-sabotage mode. Magical efforts are littered with self-doubt and second-guessing. It not only wonders if the magic will work, but begins to think that no effort performed heretofore ever really did. Before it's said and done, Pisces simply gives up. It decides to leave the magic to those more powerful, more knowledgeable, and better suited to that type of work.

Pisces Moon Affirmation

> I am the fish that swims through the sea
> Where in the Waters of Life, I stir constantly
> I am the Power and I am the Force
> Of powerful magic as I chart the course
> Of the bubbles of cauldrons and whispers of spells
> I am the Power that makes Magic gel

You've learned about your personal Moon and what it means to you magically. You've countered your pitfalls with the daily affirmations. But now that you've done the work and learned the lessons, how do you apply that information to your magic? More to the point, how can you use it to increase your magical odds?

It's not as difficult as it seems. All you need is an ephemeris, an almanac, or a calendar that charts daily information about the Moon's zodiacal cycles. (All are inexpensive and well worth the cost.) Then just schedule any difficult workings on a day when the Moon sign matches yours. When worked in this fashion, spell results are not only astounding, but quick to immediate.

What if the proper Moon sign doesn't coincide with a day of the week that's appropriate to your purpose? What then? Not to worry. Because the Moon sign is in harmony with you, the practitioner—and your emotional realm—it gives you a magical edge. This means that it's possible for projects to manifest now, even if they ordinarily would not, and that's definitely an edge we all can use!

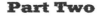

Part Two

Lunar Enchantments

A broom tied in ribbons, some stones, a lace shawl
A basket of candles, herbs hung on the wall
Incenses, oils, and a vase filled with flowers
Patiently wait as the clock ticks off hours
(Waiting till dusk gives release to the night
Waiting till stars are aloft and alight
Waiting for magic to call them to dance
Together, and manifest what was pure chance
Into reality—into conclusion—
Bringing true form to that which was illusion)
For the time when the wish and the effort are one
When the candles are lit and the spell is begun
When incense smoke curls around both herb and stone
When impossible dreams breathe a life of their own
For the time when the Full or the Crescent or Cloaked
Releases Her power as She is invoked
When they dance in the magic and set it all free
As four words are uttered: "So mote it be!"

—Dorothy Morrison

6

Waxing Moon Phase Efforts

While I usually format the grimoire sections of my books in alphabetical order, this one is set up a bit differently. The reason is that nearly any magical effort can enjoy success regardless of Moon phase, provided it's performed in a harmonious manner with that period. Take money, for example. If you really need it now (and most of us do by the time we get around to performing an appropriate spell), it simply can't wait until the Moon decides to wax. Not to worry, though. The solution is to work a spell to decrease personal poverty—or your monthly payments—during the waning Moon. You get the idea. It's just a matter of knowing how to tweak the effort so it works in harmony with the Moon phase at hand.

Therefore, this section is set up by Moon phase. To use it to your best advantage, just find the current Moon phase, then check for an appropriate spell listing.

ACCEPTANCE

Spell to Gain the Acceptance of Others

Materials

1 yellow candle

1 small vial of frankincense oil

½ teaspoon grated orange peel

Vegetable oil

Pencil

Begin by drawing two intersecting circles on the candle, then anoint it with the oil and roll it in the orange peel. Light the candle and visualize yourself being invited into the social circles, circles of friendship, or organizational circles that you desire. Once the image is firmly fixed in your mind's eye, say something like:

> *Wax and oil and herb blend well*
> *To work the magic of this spell*
> *Acceptance is what I desire*
> *And as you meld by flame of fire*
> *So I meld into the group*
> *To hold a place inside the loop*
> *Welcomed by those whom I choose*
> *Kept abreast of all the news*
> *And treated just like family*
> *As I will, so mote it be*

Place the vial of oil in front of the candle, and say something like:

Oil of Sun with golden shine
To this task you are assigned:
Bring acceptance unto me
As I wear you, let all see
That I'd make a great addition
Be my magic of ignition
Blessed by herb and flame of fire
Bring to me what I desire

Leave the vial in front of the candle until the wick extinguishes itself, then wear a few drops of the oil every day.

Wearing unakite jewelry or carrying a stone charged for personal acceptance tends to break the barriers set by others.

ATTENTION
Spell to Make People Notice You

Materials

1 orange candle

1 small magnet

1 small piece of hematite or hematite jewelry

If you're feeling somewhat inconsequential in the scheme of things, or folks just don't seem to notice you, this spell can make all the difference. Begin by lighting the candle and watching its flame dance for a few moments. Then say something like:

> *I am radiance, I am light*
> *I am the dancing flame, so bright*
> *Sparking interest where I go*
> *From all directions, high and low*

Place the magnet in front of the candle, then cover it with your hand, saying something like:

> *Magnetism currently is mine*
> *It weaves its spell like twining vine*
> *People are now drawn to me*
> *Like iron to a magnet, it shall be*

Place the stone or jewelry on top of the magnet and say something like:

> *Stone of iron ore from the ground*
> *To draw attention, you are bound*
> *As you go with me, day to day*
> *In work and business, fun and play*
> *You shall make all pay me heed—*
> *To hear my words, record my deeds*
> *And give the credit that I'm due—*
> *To these tasks, I conjure you*

Leave the objects in front of the candle until the wick burns out, then carry the stone with you or wear the jewelry.

AUTOMOBILES

Automobile Protection Spell

(While inserted here for ease of placement, this spell may be performed at any time, regardless of Moon phase.)

Visualize a blue bubble of protection emanating from the center of the vehicle and growing in size until it entirely encases the automobile. As you visualize, chant something like:

> *Sphere of magic, sphere of power*
> *Increase your potency with each hour*
> *Protect this vehicle and me*
> *As I will, so mote it be*

BALANCE

Mundane and Spiritual Balancing Bath

Materials
Baking soda
Table salt

Draw a warm bath, then toss in a handful of baking soda and a handful of salt. Stir the water clockwise with your hand to dissolve the substances, and chant something like:

> *Salt and soda, twirl throughout*
> *To bring me balance in and out*

Then sit in the tub and say:

> *Let me float between the worlds*
> *As easily as you now swirl*
> *Within this water—without strife—*
> *Bring this power to my life*
> *Total balance is my plea*
> *Do now what I ask of thee*

Totally immerse yourself in the water twice, then get out of the tub. Do not use a towel; let your body dry naturally.

When emotional balance flies out the window, wearing or carrying either a smoky quartz or a watermelon tourmaline helps to focus energy and put things back in perspective.

BANK LOANS
Spell to Obtain a Loan

Materials

1 green bayberry-scented candle
Pencil

Using the pencil, inscribe the candle with the amount of cash you need to borrow. Then light the candle and chant something like:

Candle light and candle fire
Bring to me what I desire
Bring the money that I need
By wing and foot with lightning speed

Allow the candle to burn down completely.

BEAUTY
Beautiful Skin Spell

Materials

1 white candle
1 bottle vitamin E
1 bottle vitamin A (if acne is a problem)

Light the candle and place the bottles in front of it. Enchant the vitamins by saying something like:

Vitamins, be magic tools, be conjured to this task
With each ingestion, bring my skin the beauty that I ask
Be now potent, be now strong, be what you need to be
To bring my skin new radiance and elasticity
So by the time this bottle's gone
Real beauty shall shine through
Work your magic, vitamins—do what I ask of you

Leave the bottles in front of the candle until the wick burns out, then ingest a vitamin from each bottle every morning upon rising.

BUSINESS

Spell to Ensure Successful Contracts and Proposals

Lick your finger and use it to draw a pentacle on the back of each sheet of the contract or proposal packet. Place the proposal in an envelope and draw a pentacle on its back as well, while chanting something like:

> *With spit of tongue and cell of flesh*
> *Stout magic into these sheets mesh*
> *Bring success and bring it fast*
> *So mote it be—this spell is cast*

Mail or deliver the packet on a Thursday.

Spell to Increase Business Cash Flow

Materials

1 small piece of aventurine

Hold the stone in your dominant hand and concentrate on money flowing in to your business. Enchant the stone by saying something like:

> *Money come and money grow*
> *Into my cash box gush and flow*
> *And fill it to the very top*
> *Then keep on coming—never stop*

Place the stone in the cash register or bank bag.

CHANGE

Spell to Become More Accepting of Change

Materials

1 small piece of unakite

Hold the stone in your hand and examine it carefully. Look at the color changes and see how the pink and green splotches work together effortlessly to form a beautiful work of art. Then hold the stone to your third eye and feel its power: the power of change, the power of acceptance, and the power of beauty that comes from such flexibility. Once you feel the energy flowing strongly, enchant the stone by saying something like:

> *Stone of brightest pink and green*
> *With your power, help me glean*
> *The joys that change can bring to life—*
> *In spite of its annoying strife—*
> *Help me learn to flux and flex*
> *And understand how it connects*
> *To my growth and to my goals*
> *Help me accept its many roles*
> *Help me finally to embrace*
> *Its very necessary place*
> *Within my own reality*
> *As I will, so mote it be*

Carry the stone with you, and stroke it gently when you become uncomfortable with the changes in your life.

CHARGING AND CONSECRATION

To Charge and Consecrate Stones

(While inserted here for ease of placement, this chant may be used at any time, regardless of Moon phase.)

Materials

1 candle in a color appropriate to the purpose

Stone you wish to charge and consecrate

Light the candle and hold the stone in your dominant hand. Once it begins to pulse, hold it to your third eye and visualize it aiding you in obtaining the goal you envision. Still concentrating on your goal and purpose, place the stone in front of the candle and say something like:

> *Stone of might and Earthly power*
> *Increase in strength with every hour*
> *Until you've reached full potency*
> *As I will, so mote it be*

Leave the stone there until the candle burns out, then use it toward your goal.

To Charge a Candle

(While inserted here for ease of placement, this chant may be used at any time, regardless of Moon phase.)

Materials

1 candle in a color appropriate to the purpose of the spell at hand

Light the candle, and as you gaze into the dancing flame, say:

> *As I create Light and set its flame free*
> *So does its power come back unto me*

Proceed with the spell.

To Charge an Amulet or Talisman

Materials

1 yellow candle
1 candle in a color appropriate to the purpose
An amulet or talisman
Salt

Light the candles and place the object between them. Blow on the object and say:

> *I give to you the gift of Air*
> *Stormy gales and breezes fair*

Carefully pass the object through flame of the candle that's in harmony with your purpose, and say:

> *I give to you the gift of Fire*
> *That you may work toward my desire*

Lick your finger and use it to draw a small invoking pentagram on the object, while saying:

> *With Water, I now give you life*
> *Both bubbling brooks and tidal strife*

Finally, sprinkle a few grains of salt on the object and say:

> *I fertilize you with this Earth*
> *Grow strong and thrive within Her girth*

Concentrating on the goal and purpose of the object, hold the object to your third eye and say something like:

> *I now imbue you with this power*
> *Increase in strength with every hour*
> *Until you've reached full potency*
> *As I will, so mote it be*

Leave the object between the candles until the wicks burn out, then use it toward the intended purpose.

COMMUNICATION

Spell to Get Your Point Across

Materials

1 small piece of turquoise or turquoise jewelry

Visualize yourself calmly speaking in a clear, concise manner. Then enchant the stone by saying something like:

Stone of sheer diplomacy
Make my voice heard, let all see
The point that I must make today
And clear all cloudiness away
So that it hits its mark with ease
As I will, so mote it be

Carry or wear the stone.

COMPUTERS AND PERIPHERALS

Circuit of Protection Blessing

Hold your hands over the computer or peripheral and visualize it working flawlessly. Wait until you feel the energy begin to flow between your hands and the object, then say something like:

I build an aura around you
A circuit of protection, true
By Waxing Moon it grows and thrives
Protecting jumpers, cables, drives
And every part that's capsulized
Within your body and comprise
The mechanism that you are;
A strong protection that now bars
All mishaps that might come your way
I seal you from this very day
By circuit of my energy
As I will, so mote it be

COURAGE

Charm for Courage

Materials

Ace of Swords from your favorite tarot deck

1 purple candle

Make a copy of the card by either scanning and printing, or taking it to a copy machine. Cut off the excess paper, then place the image in front of the candle and light the wick. See yourself holding the sword in your hand, and going into battle calmly and unafraid. Hold the image in your hands and empower it by saying something like:

> *Lord and Lady, Moon and Sun*
> *Elements and Ancient Ones*
> *Lend Your powers to this charm*
> *So they mix—both cool and warm—*
> *To bring the courage that I seek*
> *Bring it forth in words I speak*
> *Bring it forth in every action*
> *Until it meets Your satisfaction*
> *And every doubt slips far from me*
> *As I will, so mote it be*

Leave the image in front of the candle until the wick burns out, then carry the image with you.

★ ——————————————————————

If shyness is a problem, carry a piece of tigereye to increase self-confidence.

—————————————————————— ★

CREATIVITY

Ringing in the Muses Spell

Materials

5 small bells

1 yard each yellow, red, blue, green,
  and purple ribbon

Thread a bell on each length of ribbon, then tie the first four ribbons to tree branches in the order listed above, saying with each:

> *To ring these bells, all breezes blow*
> *Carry their sounds both high and low*
> *To wake the Muses from Their rest*
> *Heed ye now this firm request*

Then tie the purple ribbon to a branch, saying something like:

> *From East and South and West and North*
> *Muses hear me: now come forth*
> *From South and West and North and East*
> *Inspiration now release*
> *From West and North and East and South*
> *Creative powers bud and sprout*
> *From North and East and South and West*
> *Heed my call and this request*
> *As these bells ring in the breeze*
> *Let ideas flow forth with ease*
> *Bring inspiration with the wind—*
> *In constant stream without an end—*

> *Unleash Your creativity*
> *Muses, bring it now to me*

Creative blocks will begin to dissipate within twenty-four hours.

★ ───────────────────────

Anointing the temples with vanilla oil or vanilla extract clears the psychic channels for creative flow.

─────────────────────── ★

ELOQUENCE
Public Speaking Charm

(May also be used as a charm to ease stuttering.)

Materials

1 carnelian pendant (a carnelian strung on a
   silk cord may be substituted)

Hold the pendant to your mouth and visualize yourself speaking with ease and enunciating all words clearly. Then kiss the stone and hold it to your third eye, charging it by saying something like:

> *Stone of eloquence and grace*
> *From my words, all flaws erase*
> *Bring to me articulate speech*
> *Let all words be in my reach*

Grant to me now perfect diction
Let my words flow with conviction
So that I'm understood by all
Carnelian, hearken to my call

Wear the pendant for four consecutive days and nights, then put it on whenever you have to speak in public.

ENEMIES

Chant to Shield Oneself from an Enemy

For best results, say this chant three times each day for two weeks.

Space there is and space there be
Between (name of enemy) and me
By Waxing Moon this space shall grow
Until she (he) no longer causes woe
For anyone, for mine, for me
As I will, so mote it be

FERTILITY

Prayer for General Fertility

Go outdoors at dawn (or to a window where you can see both the Moon and rising Sun) and invoke Their aid by saying something like:

Goddess of the pale moonlight
Lord of Sun, so bold and bright
Lend Your power every day

To bless me in my work and play
Bless the land that is my home
Bless its animals that roam
Bless its waters and its crops
Bless stones and trees and mountain tops
Bless all who live upon this land
Bestow Your great abundance and
Fertility to all I do
This I humbly ask of You

FOCUS

Smudging Spell for Concentration

Materials

Charcoal block

Fireproof dish

2–3 sandalwood incense cones (crumbled)

½ teaspoon celery seed

Oven mitt (optional)

Light the charcoal block in the fireproof dish and scatter the incense and celery seed on top. See the smoke whisking away any scattered thoughts and energies, leaving behind only the power of concentration. Empower the burning mixture by saying something like:

Scattered energies abate
As this smoke does infiltrate
The atmosphere. Smudge, let me see
With clear and perfect clarity

The tasks that I must orchestrate
And help me now to concentrate
Blocking all else from my view
But the simple avenues
That I must follow actively
As I will, so mote it be

Hold the dish in your hand (you may want to use an oven mitt for this) and smudge yourself with the smoke to enhance your personal focus.

☆ ─────────────────────────

To ground scattered energies, carry or wear a piece of hematite.

───────────────────────── ☆

FORGIVENESS

Just Desserts Forgiveness Spell

Materials

A slice of your favorite cake

To become more forgiving (this is important if you happen to be a grudge-holder), place your hands over the cake and visualize a pink light flowing from them. Allow the light to envelope the dish and saturate the contents. Then enchant the cake further by saying something like:

Forgiveness is the sweetest thing that one can ever bake
So I impart that quality right now unto this cake

> *Every crumb is saturated—*
> *Coated through and through—*
> *But by pinkest light and sheerest will its*
> *Power still accrues*
> *So with every forkful I ingest, this quality's consumed*
> *And blocks out everything that keeps from*
> *Bringing it to bloom*
> *And as I eat the final bite, forgiveness then will play*
> *Within my heart and on my lips forever and a day*

Eat the cake and feel the power of forgiveness grow within you.

GAMBLING

Gambling Wash

Materials

1 cup boiling water
1 tablespoon chamomile

Pour the water over the chamomile and watch the herb begin to color the water as you say something like:

> *Herb in water, steep as tea*
> *Become a lucky wash for me*
> *So whatever you shall soak*
> *Will good gambling luck invoke*

When the tea cools, strain out the herb and store the liquid in a jar in the refrigerator. Just before going out to gamble, rub a few drops between your hands and on any money in your wallet.

★ ————————————————

For additional luck in games of chance, carry a piece of aventurine and a piece of pyrite in your left pants pocket.

———————————————— ★

GOALS

Goal Manifestation Spell

Materials
Paper and pen
Red marking pen
Highlighting pen (any color)
1 yellow candle

Draw a picture of a road that forks in many directions, but leads to the same end. (Don't worry if you're not an artist; this drawing doesn't have to be anything fancy.) Examine the picture and mark the straightest route with the highlighting pen, then write your goal along that route with the red pen.

Light the candle and see yourself traveling directly down the correct path to attaining your goal. Place the map in front of the candle and say something like:

> *Radiant Mother in the sky*
> *Light my journey from on high*

> *Guide me with your silver glow*
> *So the proper path I'll know—*
> *The path of true accomplishment;*
> *The path for which my dreams are meant—*
> *And with that guidance, please allow*
> *That I may manifest them now*
> *And bring them to reality*
> *As I will, so mote it be*

Leave the map in front of the candle until the wick burns out, then carry the map with you.

HEALTH/HEALING

Spell to Ensure Good Health

Materials

1 glass of water

Place a hand on both sides of the glass and visualize the water forming a river of health-protection that travels through your body as you drink it. Then stir the water clockwise with your index finger, saying something like:

> *Waters of Life, Waters of Love*
> *Both on surface and above*
> *I stir you up as a remedy*
> *To keep my good health problem-free*
> *Grow in power and in strength*
> *So as you travel your course's length*

You'll wash out all impurity

As I will, so mote it be

Drink the water, and repeat the spell daily.

HOME

Spell to Sell a Home

Materials

1 green candle

1 match

1 sheet white paper

1 hair from a family pet or your head

1 small feather

1 12-inch length of purple ribbon or yarn

Water

Light the candle with the match, then put the match aside for later use. Visualize serious buyers looking at the house, receiving your asking price, and the contracts being signed. Then place the sheet of paper in front of the candle, and lay the hair in the center, saying:

By fur of mammal from the Earth

Place the burned match on top, saying:

By dancing Flame of joy and mirth

Place the feather on top, saying:

By feathered friend upon the Breeze

Place a drop of water on top, saying:

> *By fin and scale in deepest Seas*
> *I conjure You to work as one*
> *To sell this house till it is done*
> *To bring prospective buyers here*
> *Make them come from far and near*
> *But cast off those imperious*
> *And only bring the serious*
> *Who have the cash and have the means*
> *To qualify; and intervene*
> *To get the price that I now ask*
> *Hurry now unto this task*

Fold all four edges of the paper to form a parcel, seal the ingredients inside, then secure it with the ribbon by tying nine knots. Say one line with each knot:

> *By knot of one, the spell's begun*
> *By knot of two, the magic's true*
> *By knot of three, the magic's free*
> *By knot of four, it opens doors*
> *By knot of five, it breathes new life*
> *By knot of six, the magic's fixed*
> *By knot of seven, it reaches heaven*
> *By knot of eight, my wish is fate*
> *By knot of nine, results are mine*

Leave the packet in front of the candle until the wick extinguishes itself, then bury it by the front door of the house you wish to sell.

Spell to Purchase the Home of Your Dreams

Materials

1 purple candle

Newspaper ad or listing of the home you want

1 yellow handkerchief or a 4-by-4-inch square of
yellow fabric

Taglock from the property (a blade of grass, a paint
chip, or even lint from the inside of the house
works well)

Paper on which you've written your financial offer
(be realistic)

1 12-inch length of purple ribbon

Light the candle and see yourself living in the house you
desire. Place the ad or listing on top of the cloth (it's
okay to fold it if you need to) and say:

> *This is my home*
> *It's mine alone*

Place the taglock on top, saying:

> *By tag of space*
> *I claim this place*

Place the paper with your financial offer on top and say:

> *This is the very price I'll pay*
> *Other offers shall be cast away*

Gather the edges of the cloth together and secure with
the ribbon by tying nine knots (use the instructions for

the knot chant listed in "Spell to Sell a Home"). Visualize yourself owning the home as you tie each knot.

Leave the pouch in front of the candle until the wick burns out, then call for an appointment to see the house. Hide the pouch somewhere on the property. (Closets and pantries make great hiding places.)

INCENSE

Waxing Moon Incense

Materials
⅛ teaspoon camphor

2 teaspoons dried wormwood or patchouli

Charcoal block

Mix the camphor and wormwood during the Waxing Moon, then charge the incense by saying something like:

> *As Moon increases in the night*
> *I free your power to take flight*
> *And bring the things I ask of thee*
> *As I will, so mote it be*

Burn on a charcoal block.

INSPIRATION

To Enlist the Aid of the Muses

Materials

1 yellow candle

Vanilla oil

Thyme

Anoint the candle with oil, then roll it in the thyme. Light the candle while chanting something like:

> *Muses come from near and far*
> *Hear my call from where you are*
> *Propose, inspire, enchant, enthuse*
> *Until I am at last infused*
> *With new ideas and clear directive*
> *Fill me with a fresh perspective*

Let the candle burn down completely.

JOBS

Treasure-Mapping Spell for the Perfect Job

Materials

A collection of old magazines and newspapers

1 large piece white poster board

1 orange candle

Scissors

Glue

Paper and colored pens (optional)

The idea here is to make a collage of everything that you're looking for in the perfect job, so begin by going through the magazines and newspapers, cutting out any related pictures and words. If you can't find everything you're looking for, it's perfectly permissible to just draw the pictures or write the words on paper and cut them out. When you're sure you've collected everything necessary to depict your perfect job, arrange the cutouts on the poster board and glue them down.

Place the poster in front of the altar and light the orange candle, saying something like:

> *Flame of fire, now dancing bright*
> *Orange candle, with your light*
> *Attract the job initiated*
> *Bring to me what I've created*
> *Waste no time now with this task*
> *Bring swift results; the spell is cast*

Leave the poster in front of the altar until the candle burns out, then hang it in a spot where you'll see it several times each day.

⭐ ─────────────────────────

To increase your chances of getting a job, wear power colors like black, red, or purple to interviews.

─────────────────────────── ⭐

JUDGMENT

Chant for Sound Decision-Making

Sit in a comfortable position in a quiet place outdoors and examine your problem from every angle. If no solution presents itself within the first five minutes, ask the Moon for guidance in making a decision by saying something like:

> *O Moon Who grows more every night*
> *Come and guide me with Your light*
> *Show me now what You envision*
> *As a fair and sound decision*
> *So my choice won't bring despair*
> *And I know what's truly fair*
> *Waxing Moon, now hear my plea*
> *Do now what I ask of Thee*

Kiss your hand to the Moon three times and wait. The help you seek will present itself.

KNOWLEDGE

Knowledge Retention Charm

Materials

1 purple or lavender candle

Vegetable oil

¼ teaspoon powdered spikenard

1 small piece fluorite

Anoint the candle with vegetable oil, then roll it in the spikenard. Light the candle and hold the stone to your third eye. See yourself retaining all that you read, hear, and see. Then charge the stone by saying something like:

> *Mighty fluorite—student's stone—*
> *I ask you now these skills to hone:*
> *A clarity of knowledge gained*
> *That all I read may be retained*
> *As well as what I see and hear*
> *Bring understanding—make it clear—*
> *So all that's placed in front of me*
> *Is retained as it should be*

Leave the stone in front of the candle until the wick extinguishes itself, then carry the stone with you.

LEADERSHIP

Charm to Increase Leadership Skills

Materials

1 purple candle

¼ teaspoon dried yarrow flowers

¼ teaspoon celery seed

¼ teaspoon dried sage

1 bay leaf

1 small piece of tigereye

1 4-by-4-inch square of purple fabric

Vegetable oil

Anoint the candle with oil and roll it in the thyme. Light the candle and place the fabric in front of it. Spend a few moments visualizing yourself in the capacity of leader, having good skills, and excellent judgment. Then call on the Maiden by saying something like:

> *Maiden Goddess, turn about*
> *And cast Your eyes on me throughout*
> *The day and night, and help me see*
> *What a leader needs to be*

Sprinkle the yarrow in the center of the fabric and say something like:

> *Herb of courage, skill and war*
> *To this task, your strengths impart*

Add the celery seed, saying something like:

> *Herb of mental powers, rare*
> *Help me think things through with care*

Add the sage, saying something like:

> *Sage, impart your wisdom, too*
> *So I know just what to do*

Add the bay leaf, saying something like:

> *Bay leaf, add your victory*
> *So of failure, I'll be free*

Finally, add the tigereye, saying something like:

> *Stone of leaders, stone of strength*
> *Hone the skills I need at length*

> *So a good leader, I shall be*
> *As I will, so mote it be*

Leave the cloth and ingredients on the altar until the candle burns out, then tie the ends of the square securely while saying something like:

> *O Maiden Goddess, bless this charm*
> *So that none surface to bring harm*
> *To those I lead by day or night*
> *Watch over me and with Your light*
> *Guide my hand and heart and tongue*
> *So with this charm I shall become*
> *A leader of great quality*
> *As I will, so mote it be*

Carry the charm with you.

LEGAL MATTERS
Spell to Win Favor in Court

Materials

1 yellow candle

1 small double-terminated citrine

1 tablespoon dried chamomile

1 bay leaf

1 5-by-5-inch square of yellow fabric

(Add 1 tablespoon cinnamon if you are seeking a monetary settlement)

Light the candle and see the scales of justice tipping in your favor. Place the fabric square in front of the candle and place the stone on top. Place your dominant hand on the stone and say something like:

> *Stone of balance and success*
> *I conjure you unto this quest*
> *Let the scales of justice tip*
> *In my favor as they dip*
> *And let all see that I deserve*
> *Success in court without reserve*

Sprinkle the chamomile on top of the stone, and cover it with the bay leaf while saying something like:

> *Potent herbs, I conjure you*
> *Infuse this charm with power, true*
> *Bring the scales to tip with ease*
> *Bring victory unto me, please*
> *So when it's all been said and done*
> *There is no doubt that I have won*

Tie the ends of the fabric together to secure the contents, saying something like:

> *To win in court is now your task*
> *I leave you by this flame to bask*
> *And absorb its ever growing power*
> *Increase in potency with each hour*

Leave the pouch in front of the candle until the wick burns out. Carry the pouch to court with you.

LOVE
Love-Attracting Potpourri

Materials

2 tablespoons dried, crushed rose petals
(preferably red and/or pink)

1 teaspoon powdered cinnamon
or 1 crushed cinnamon stick

½ teaspoon cloves

½ teaspoon allspice

½ teaspoon dried orange peel

6 drops vanilla oil

Mix all the ingredients together while seeing your perfect love being drawn to you like a magnet. Then place your hands over the mixture, palms down, saying something like:

> *Come to me now, perfect love*
> *By Sea, by Earth, by Sky above*
> *Feel the Spark now in your heart*
> *As this essence now imparts*
> *Knowledge of my presence here*
> *Come at once to me, my dear*

Repeat the chant five more times, then pour the mixture in a bowl and place it in your bedroom. Alternatively, use the mixture as a simmering potpourri by adding one tablespoon to a small pot of water.

Charm for True Love

Materials

1 red candle

1 pink candle

1 small piece rose quartz

6 strands of your hair

1 tablespoon love-attracting potpourri
(see instructions on page 168)

Red charm bag

Light the candles and visualize your true love coming to you. See both of you enjoying a loving, romantic, and fun-filled life together. Then place the stone in the bag, saying something like:

> *Stone of love, now be a guide*
> *Bring my true love to my side*
> *Be a beacon day and night*
> *Bring my true love into sight*

Place the strands of hair in the bag and say something like:

> *Six strands of hair, I offer, too*
> *To draw the one whose heart is true*
> *That she (he) shall know but with one glance*
> *That we were meant for true romance*

Place the potpourri in the bag and say its related chant, then place the bag between the candles until the wicks burn out. Carry the bag with you.

LOST ITEMS

Chant to Retrieve Missing Objects

Visualize the missing object and see yourself finding it easily and quickly. Then firmly and loudly, say something like:

> *Keepers of the great abyss*
> *Of cosmic holes and things amiss*
> *Bring what's lost now back to me*
> *Loose your hold and set it free*

LUCK

Lucky Horseshoe Home Charm

Materials

1 cup boiling water

1 tablespoon dried chamomile

1 horseshoe

Paintbrush

Pour the boiling water over the chamomile and allow it to steep until cool. Then paint the horseshoe with the tea, covering both sides, while saying something like:

> *Lucky shoe with points turned up*
> *Let good fortune fill my cup*
> *Attract and draw it—bring it here—*
> *So that this home is filled with cheer*
> *Let it flow herein throughout*
> *A steady stream from the Cosmic spout*

Bring good fortune now to me
As I will, so mote it be

Repeat the painting and chanting twice more, then dry
the shoe thoroughly. Hang it above the front door with
the points turned up to the ceiling.

☆ ————————————————————

Carry or wear an apache tear to draw
good luck all year 'round.

———————————————————— ☆

LUST

Lingerie Charm to Intensify Lust

Materials
9 whole cloves
1 old sock (must be clean)
New red lingerie or underwear

Wash the lingerie or underwear on the delicates cycle, but
shut the machine off before the final rinse. Tuck the cloves
inside the sock and knot the end to secure them. Place the
sock inside the washer and turn it back on, saying:

With lust, this clothing I imbue
By herb and water, it's infused
To stir the spark and kindle fire
To bring that which I desire

When the cycle's finished, set the drier to its lowest setting, then toss in the lingerie and sock. As the items begin to rotate, envision yourself embroiled in the throes of hot, passionate lovemaking, and say something like:

> *By heat and spark and flame of fire*
> *I kindle passion and desire*
> *I kindle lust—its dance within—*
> *And also in this spell I spin*
> *Uninhibited sex that's free*
> *When I wear this, it shall be*

When the lingerie is dry, put it on and prepare for an exciting encounter.

MAGICAL EMPOWERMENT
Magic-Boosting Bath Mixture

Materials

1 tablespoon mugwort

¼ teaspoon allspice

⅛ teaspoon vanilla extract

Paper coffee filter

Purple ribbon or yarn

Place the mugwort and allspice in the coffee filter, then sprinkle the vanilla extract on top. Gather the edges of the filter and secure it tightly with the ribbon. Place your hands over the pouch and empower the mixture by saying something like:

> *By extract, leaf, and powdered seed*
> *I conjure you to work with speed*
> *To boost the magic that I claim*
> *And speed results for which I aim*
> *Bring your power now to me*
> *As I will, so mote it be*

Toss the bag into your bath. Allow your body to dry naturally, then perform any necessary spell work.

MEDITATION

Premeditation Prayer to the Bright Maiden

> *Maiden of the Waxing Moon*
> *With my mind, please now attune*
> *And bring the answers that I seek*
> *Bring them clearly so they speak*
> *Their true meaning unto me*
> *As I will, so mote it be*

MONEY

Spell to Increase Cash Flow

Materials

1 small piece of aventurine

1 dollar bill

Green embroidery floss or ribbon

Place the stone in the center of the bill and visualize large amounts of money flowing directly into your hands. Then enchant the objects by saying something like:

> *Stone and currency of power*
> *Your many blessings on me shower*
> *Bring money to me—let it flow*
> *Into my hands, then make it grow*
> *Until my need is quenched at last*
> *Cash and stone, do what I ask*

Fold the bill around the stone and secure it with the floss or ribbon. Then place the packet in your purse or carry it with your pocket change.

NIGHTMARES

To Empower a Dream Catcher

Materials
1 purple candle
Dream catcher

Light the candle and hold the dream catcher in front of it. Visualize a powerful purple aura surrounding the dream catcher. Once the image is firmly fixed in your mind's eye, enchant the object by saying something like:

> *Perfect web in circle round*
> *By this spell you now are bound*
> *To keep all nightmares far from those*
> *Within your charge while they may doze*
> *And bring forth pleasant dreams to all*
> *Within your keep when sleep does fall*

By purple aura and its strength
This spell is infinite in length

Leave the dream catcher in front of the candle until the wick burns out, then hang the dream catcher over your bed.

PHYSICAL ENERGY
Energy-Increasing Charm

Materials

1 small clear quartz crystal

Hold the stone in your hand until you feel it begin to pulse. See yourself with more than enough energy to accomplish your tasks without being tired. Then empower the stone by saying something like:

Stone of power unsurpassed
By this spell that I now cast
Revitalize my body now
Energize it as I plow
Through all the things that I must do
Bring energy to my mind, too
So that I don't tire easily
As I will, so mote it be

Carry the stone with you.

PRODUCTIVITY
Spell for a Productive Work Day

Materials

1 hematite

1 quartz crystal

1 orange calcite

Small basket or ash tray

Place the hematite in the basket and enchant it by saying:

> *Ground and heal, magnetic one*
> *Bring clarity till day is done*

Add the quartz crystal and say:

> *Bring boundless energy my way*
> *And let it last all through the day*

Add the calcite and say:

> *Stone of joy and yellow light*
> *Help me sort through workday plight*

Place the container of stones on your desk and say:

> *Help me work till I am done*
> *Bring inspiration on the run*
> *So that when the day is through*
> *I have nothing left to do*

PROTECTION
Magical Protection Bubble

When you need protection, see yourself as being encased in a large bubble that moves about as you do. Then call on the protection of the Goddess by saying something like:

> *Goddess Mother hear my prayer*
> *Keep me safely in Your care*
> *Until all harm has passed away*
> *Watch over me throughout this day*

Know that you are safe and that the bubble will disappear when you're out of harm's way.

TRAVEL
Charm for Safe Travel

Materials

1 yellow candle

1 teaspoon lavender

1 teaspoon chamomile

1 small piece of amethyst

1 8-by-8-inch square of purple fabric

1 small piece of amethyst

Light the candle and place the fabric square in front of it with a corner toward the candle so it looks like a diamond. Sprinkle the lavender in the center of the fabric, saying something like:

> *Protective herb, I call on You*
> *Lend Your power and imbue*
> *Our travels with Your safe embrace*
> *As we go from place to place*

Sprinkle the chamomile on top and say something like:

> *Herb of fortune, hear my plea*
> *Lend Your good luck now to me*
> *Smile on us where e're we go*
> *And keep us far from harm and woe*

Place the stone on top of the herbs and say something like:

> *With amethyst, I set the spell*
> *So all travels shall go well*
> *So stress and problems cannot call*
> *And Your powers aid us, one and all*

Tie the top and bottom corners of the fabric square together, saying:

> *From North to South, I seal the spell*

Then tie the two remaining corners together, saying:

> *From West to East, it's sealed as well*
> *To all who travel now with me*
> *Grant your great security*
> *Protect us all while we're away*
> *By Moon of night and Sun of day*

Leave the parcel in front of the candle until the wick burns out, then carry the charm on your person while traveling.

VICTORY

Spell to Become Victorious

Materials

1 purple candle
1 bay leaf
Purple marking pen
Fireproof dish

Light the candle, then stand facing North while visualizing yourself being the victor in the situation at hand. Visualize a transparent green star in front of you. See its arms extending closer and closer until it wraps itself around your body and completely envelops you. See a transparent red star at your back and repeat the visualization. Repeat the process with a transparent yellow star at your right, and a blue one at your left. Finally, see a clear star at your head and allow it to totally encase your body. (You may feel a slight tingle with the last star. Don't worry. This is normal.)

Using the marking pen, write the word "victory" on the bay leaf. Using the candle flame, set the bay leaf on fire, then place it in the fireproof dish to burn, saying something like:

By North and South, by East and West
By Spirit, too, I now am blessed
By bay, whose laurels signify
A contest won beneath the sky
Work to bring what I request:
This victory; and do not rest
Until You've brought it back to me
As I will, so mote it be

When the ashes are cool, toss them on the winds.

WAR

To Ensure the Safe Return of Soldiers

Materials

1 bay leaf for each soldier you wish to include
Purple indelible marking pen

Using the marker, write the name of each soldier on a
bay leaf. See him or her returning home safely and in
good spirits. Then, still focusing on the soldier's safety,
drop the leaves, one by one, into running water. As you
drop each one, say:

I give You, Water, this request
This soldier sails now as your guest
And as your charge; so with this spell
Unto the Universe propel
This magic; then with haste please bring
Her (him) safely home with neither sting

Of fear nor grief nor casualty
As I will, so mote it be

WILLPOWER
Spell for Self-Control

Materials

1 teal or purple candle

Acorn

Light the candle and see yourself with enough willpower to resist even the strongest urges. Hold the acorn in your dominant hand until you feel its power begin to pulse. Then charge the acorn by saying something like:

Seed of oak and seed of strength
Bring me self-control at length
Help keep cravings well at bay
Toss harmful urges far away
Boost my will and bring it power
Increasing it with every hour
So that this strength flows easily
As I will, so mote it be

Leave the acorn in front of the candle until the wick burns out, then carry the acorn with you.

WISDOM
Charm for Wisdom

Materials

1 purple candle

1 white handkerchief

1 small piece of amethyst

¼ teaspoon dried sage

Light the candle and see yourself becoming aware of everything going on around you. Visualize yourself seeing both sides of every situation and knowing what to do in each case. Unfold the handkerchief and place it in front of the candle. Hold the stone in your dominant hand, wait for it to pulse with energy, then hold it to your third eye, saying something like:

> *Stone of wisdom, stone of power*
> *Bring to me this very hour*
> *Acute awareness and insight*
> *And understanding of each plight*
> *That presents itself to me*
> *Bring knowledge of how things should be*
> *Let your guidance be concise*
> *So I can offer sound advice*
> *To those who seem to lose their way*
> *Stone, begin this very day*

Sprinkle the sage on top of the stone and say something like:

Prudent herb, whose name means "wise"
Work with this stone to magnify
The strength imparted to this task
So all details shall be unmasked
So I shall have a crystal view
So nothing can be misconstrued
Bring your wisdom to me, sage
And let it grow with time and age
Bring now what I ask of thee
As I will, so mote it be

Tie the ends of the handkerchief together and leave the pouch in front of the candle until the wick burns out. Carry the charm with you.

Carrying or wearing a piece of chrysocolla or sugilite opens personal channels so that wisdom may flow from all sources.

WISHES

Magical Wishing Bowl

Materials

1 white candle

1 glass or metal salad bowl

Coins

Secure the candle to the center of the bowl by melting a bit of the wax on the bottom. Then light the candle and say something like:

> *A wishing bowl, you now become*
> *A magic tool by Moon and Sun*
> *With curving shape, by light of fire*
> *To bring to me what I desire*

Then place a coin in the bowl, saying something like:

> *By coin of one, this spell's begun*

Place a second coin in the bowl, saying something like:

> *By coin of two, the power brews*

Place a third coin in the bowl, saying something like:

> *By coin of three, pay heed to me*

Finally, hold your hands over the bowl on either side of the candle and say:

> *Coins be seeds to feed the power*
> *So wishes sought will bud and flower*
> *By light of fire you now are blessed*
> *And fertilized to manifest*
> *All wishes that come forth from me*
> *As I will, so mote it be*

Let the candle burn for a few minutes while seeing the power of the wish bowl increasing, then blow it out.

Light the candle every day and add a few more coins. Repeat the last chant and continue to visualize the power growing.

When you need to manifest a wish, remove one of the coins and bury it in the ground (the soil of a houseplant will work in a pinch) while visualizing your wish coming true and saying something like:

> *To the Earth now you must go*
> *To germinate and sprout and grow*
> *Into that which I require*
> *And manifest what I desire*

Replace the candle as necessary. When the bowl is full of money, take all but three coins and apply it to your favorite charity or use it for something service-oriented.

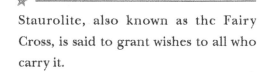

Staurolite, also known as the Fairy Cross, is said to grant wishes to all who carry it.

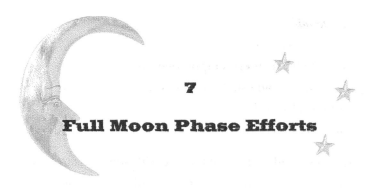

7

Full Moon Phase Efforts

Because virtually any magical goal is attainable during the Full Moon, I've reserved this section for Esbat workings. And that being the case, the following spells are listed in alphabetical order by topic with the Full Moon Esbat specific to the subject matter beneath. However, this is in no way meant to be an indicator that the spells in this section must be performed on specific Full Moons to work properly. The arrangement is simply a convenience to those who wish to incorporate magical operations into their Full Moon Circles.

CHANGE

Charm for Change and Transformation

(For best results, perform this spell on the Mead/Honey Moon. Good results can also be obtained during the Waxing Moon.)

Materials

1 purple candle

Egg shells, feathers, empty cocoons,
    empty cicada shells, and so on

Strand of your hair

Small cloth charm bag

Light the candle, then fill the bag with some of the transformative gifts of nature. Add a strand of your hair, close the bag, and place it in front of the candle, saying something like:

> *Gifts of Nature, bring a change*
> *And with it, bring this goal in range:*
> *To transform my life into what it should be*
> *To reinvent my personal reality*
> *Bring the courage I need to start life anew*
> *Transformative gifts, I ask this of You*

Leave the charm bag in front of the candle until the wick burns out, then carry the bag with you.

CHARGING AND CONSECRATION

General Empowerment for Herbs

(For best results, perform this spell on the Wort Moon. Good results can also be obtained during the Waxing Moon.)

Materials

Herbs and other plant material to be used in magic

Small bowl for each herb

Place each type of herb in a separate bowl. Charging one bowl at a time, hold your hands over the plant material until you feel its energy rise. Then run your fingers through the herbs, which should be tingling with energy by now, and chant:

> *Little plants of greatest power*
> *Increase in potency with each hour.*
> *I extend your life. I conjure your strength.*
> *I give you depth of infinite length*
> *I charge you with magical energy*
> *As I will, so mote it be*

CHILDBIRTH

Spell to Ease Delivery

Materials

¼ teaspoon lavender flowers

1 white or yellow seven-day candle

Sprinkle the lavender on top of the candle, then light the wick. Visualize the person for whom you're performing this work in the delivery room, then enlist the Mother's help by saying something like:

> *Mother Who must birth the Sun*
> *When each year is nearly done*

> *Please lend your aid unto this task*
> *An easy childbirth I do ask*
> *In little time with little pain*
> *But let the baby's strength not wane*
> *Bring all safely through this task*
> *Mother do now what I ask*

Let the candle burn all the way down.

✦ ————————————————————

Burning a mixture of lavender and roses
in the birthing room is also said to ease
labor pains and speed delivery.

———————————————————— ✦

COMPASSION

Chant to the Lord and Lady for General Compassion

(For best results, perform this spell on the Dyad Moon.
Good results can also be obtained during the Waxing
Moon.)

> *Lord and Lady, I ask that you fashion*
> *My heart to reflect Your love and compassion*
> *Allow me to feel for folks that which I should*
> *Allow me to truly see all that is good*
> *Then help me to act on what's seen and felt*
> *As You open my heart—and with love, let it melt—*

So that I may soothe all the hurt in the world
As a tool of Your love, flowing free and unfurled.

COURAGE

Bay Leaf Courage Charm

(For best results, perform this spell on the Wolf Moon. Good results can also be obtained during the Waxing Moon.)

Materials
1 bay leaf

Hold a bay leaf over your heart. Once you feel your heart beating with regularity, charge the leaf by saying something like:

> *Little leaf of victory*
> *Bring courage quickly unto me*
> *Instill it deep within my core*
> *And let it grow and thrive and soar*

Carry the leaf with you.

To gain the courage to speak your mind, string a tonka bean on a cord and wear it around your neck.

FRIENDSHIP

Spell to Gain New Friends

(For best results, perform this spell on the Dyad Moon. Good results can also be obtained during the Waxing Moon.)

Materials

1 orange candle

A few drops of lemon juice

1 small piece of chrysoprase or turquoise

Anoint the candle with the lemon juice. When the candle is dry, light the wick and hold the stone to your third eye. See yourself surrounded by wonderful people who have your best interest at heart, then enlist the aid of the Lord and Lady by saying something like:

> *Lord and Lady, hear my plea*
> *And bring new friends at once to me*
> *Strengthen old relationships*
> *And offer fresh companionship*
> *To widen my circle of laughter and fun—*
> *And moral support when battles aren't won—*
> *Make for me some strong connections*
> *And guide good friends in my direction*

Leave the stone in front of the candle until the wick burns out, then carry the stone with you.

FORGIVENESS

Spell for Cultivating Forgiveness

(For best results, perform this spell on the Hare Moon. Good results can also be obtained during the Waxing Moon.)

Materials

1 pink candle

1 package large, easy-to-grow seeds (basil, sweet pea, beans, or sunflower seeds work well for this)

Light the candle and close your eyes. See the candle flame as a tiny light dancing inside your Spirit, growing stronger and larger until it fills you not only with the capacity to forgive, but the *willingness* to do so. Then hold the seeds to your heart and bless them with this attribute by saying something like:

> *I name you for forgiveness that dances in this flame*
> *It's conjured now within your core, as my core,*
> *Too, it claims*
> *So as you germinate and grow, forgiveness grows in me*
> *Until it fills my spirit past its full capacity*
> *And spills forth from my very core and issues*
> *From my heart*
> *You are forgiveness, little seeds; your magic*
> *Now impart*

Leave the seeds in front of the candle until the wick burns out, then plant the seeds. Remember to tend them, for as they grow, forgiveness will grow in you as well.

GARDENING
Planting Chant

(For best results, perform this spell on the Hare Moon. Good results can also be obtained during the Waxing Moon.)

When planting seedlings or introducing new plants to the garden area, ensure their growth by chanting over each one:

> *Grow, my friend, your roots dig deep*
> *Into the soil, and do not sleep;*
> *Grow, instead, both lush and tall*
> *On sturdy stem with leaves that sprawl*

Plant each in the ground and tend them as necessary.

Garden and Household Plant Fertilizer Charge

(For best results, perform this spell on the Dyad Moon. Good results can also be obtained during the Waxing Moon.)

Hold your hands over fertilizer sticks and garden fertilizer, then bless and charge them for fertility by saying something like:

> *Lord and Lady, Moon and Sun*
> *I call on You, too, Ancient Ones*
> *Lend Your fertile energy*
> *To all that rests here before me*
> *So plants will grow both lush and tall*
> *When fed with these; now heed my call*

Seed Blessing

(For best results, perform this spell on the Seed Moon. Good results can also be obtained during the Waxing Moon.)

Materials
1 green candle
Seed packets

Light the candle and place the seed packets in front of it. Place your hands, palms down, over the seeds, and wait until you can feel the packets pulse with energy. Then bless the seeds by saying something like:

> *Wake from sleep now, little seeds*
> *The Sun is shining just for thee*
> *Yawn and stretch—it's time to sow*
> *You in the Earth so you may grow*
> *Lush and green; you now are bound*
> *To thriving magic in the ground*

Leave the packets in front of the candle until the wick burns out, then plant the seeds according to the package directions.

HANDFASTING/WEDDING
Prayer to Secure Marital Happiness

(For best results, use this invocation on the Dyad Moon or during the marriage ceremony itself. Good results can also be obtained during the Waxing Moon.)

Glorious Lady of the night
Passionate Lord of warmth and light
Who dance across the planet Earth
Sharing laughter, joy, and mirth
Pouring out Your love on all
Who sing Your tune and hear Your call
Bless the marriage of we (these) two
With happiness, our (their) lives imbue
And grant our (their) love shall mirror Yours—
That steadfast love that can endure
Life's mishaps, its trials and tears
As well as joy—and through the years
That we (they) grow in love, both soul and heart
And to this union, please impart
The ecstasy of passion's play
The joy of living every day
Together, as we (they) dance as one
In the magic of both Moon and Sun

INCENSE
Full Moon Incense

Materials

⅛ teaspoon anise

1 teaspoon lavender

1 teaspoon rosemary

Charcoal block

Mix the herbs during the Full Moon, then charge the incense by saying something like:

> *By pregnant Moon that lights the night*
> *I free your power to take flight*
> *And bring the things I ask of thee*
> *As I will, so mote it be*

Burn on a charcoal block.

JOY

Prayer to the Maiden to Bring Joy to Life

(For best results, say this prayer on the Chaste Moon. Good results can also be obtained during the Waning Moon.)

> *O Maiden of pubescent joy*
> *I call You forth to now destroy*
> *All fear and stress, all angst and strain*
> *All energies that cause me pain*
> *And leave within that empty space*
> *Your wondrous childlike joy and grace*
> *Your happiness, Your smiling face*
> *So that my heart is light and free*
> *By Your Name, so mote it be*

A piece of chrysoprase, when charged for joy and carried in the pocket, tends to lighten the severity of any situation.

LOVE
Spell to Find True Love

(For best results, perform this spell on the Dyad Moon. Good results can also be obtained during the Waxing Moon.)

Materials

1 red candle

1 pink candle

1 tablespoon crushed dried rose petals

1 red rose, fresh

Vegetable oil

Anoint the candles with oil and roll them in the dried petals. Then place the candles side by side with the fresh rose between them. Light the pink candle and visualize yourself caught up in the romance of the century. Do not put a face on your love. Instead, visualize your love from the back. Holding the image in your mind's eye, say something like:

Romantic love, I call to you
Bring to me a love that's true
A gentle love, a perfect one
A love who's there when day is done
A love whom I can't live without
I conjure you to search throughout
And bring just what I ask to me
As I will, so mote it be

Light the red candle and visualize yourself in the throes of wild, hot, passionate sex with your new love. Again, be careful not to add a face to this person. Holding the image in your mind's eye, say something like:

> *Passionate love, I call to you*
> *Bring to me a love that's true*
> *Filled with ardor and desire*
> *A love that burns with passion's fire*
> *A love that I can't live without*
> *I conjure you to search throughout*
> *And bring just what I ask to me*
> *As I will, so mote it be*

Pick up the rose and touch it to each candle, then say something like:

> *Red and pink, work as a team*
> *Work as one to bring my dream*
> *Find my true and perfect love*
> *The one that fits me like a glove*
> *And bring that person back to me*
> *As I will, so mote it be*

Let the candles burn out, but leave the rose where it is until it dries out. Pluck the petals loose and toss them into running water.

LUCK

Witches' Ladder for General Good Fortune

(For best results, perform this spell on the Mead/Honey Moon. Good results can also be obtained during the Waxing Moon.)

Materials

1 yard each red, white, and black ¼-inch ribbon

9 bird feathers of different colors

1 orange candle

Quick-drying glue (optional)

Braid the ribbons together and knot both ends, then attach the feathers by knotting them at equal intervals in the braid, adding a drop of glue to secure them if you wish. Enchant each feather with a particular characteristic as you knot it. While attaching a green feather, for example, you might spell it for prosperity by saying something like:

> *Financial gain now comes to me*
> *As I will, so mote it be*

On the other hand, a blue feather might be enchanted for peace and tranquility by saying something like:

> *Blue of tranquility, bring me peace*
> *By this knot, all stresses cease*

You get the idea.

Once all the feathers are attached, tie the ends of the braid in a bow. Light the candle, place the feathers in front of it, and say something like:

> *Feathered circlet, braid of three*
> *Bring good fortune unto me*
> *I conjure you unto this task*
> *Work now, ring—do as I ask*

Leave the circlet in front of the candle until the wick burns out, then hang it in an inconspicuous spot in your home.

MAGICAL EMPOWERMENT
Magical Seed Necklace

(For best results, perform this spell on the Barley Moon. Good results can also be obtained during the Waxing Moon.)

Materials
1–2 cups large soft-shelled seeds (pumpkin or
   sunflower seeds work well for this)
1 yellow candle
Hot water
Needle and thread

Soak the seeds in hot water to soften them a bit (about twenty minutes should do the trick). Light the candle and sit in front of it while you string the seeds into a necklace. When you are done, knot the thread and place the necklace in front of the candle. Enchant the necklace by saying something like:

Seeds of life, now magic's tool
Container of the cycle's rule
That sprout as plants and bear the fruit
That goes to seed, then leaf and root
That lives and dies and lives again
A reminder that life has no end
That I have strung in circle round
To complete the cycles that were bound
About you since you first were born
Come aid me now within this form
Increase my magic, bring it power,
Let it blossom full and flower
And in return, I'll give you back
Unto the Earth, so rich and black

Leave the necklace in front of the candle until the wick extinguishes itself, then wear the necklace whenever you perform magic.

Keep the necklace for a year, then bury it in the ground. Make a new necklace to replace it.

MONEY

Money Charging Chant

(For best results, perform this spell on the Dyad Moon. Good results can also be obtained during the Waxing Moon.)

To charge your change with the power of multiplication, hold it in both hands and visualize it growing in quantity, then say something like:

By Fertile Maiden, coins now grow
In quantity and number flow
Into my hands and purse and home
Into my life now, you must roam
And multiply with ease as well
I charge you, change, by rhyme of spell

NEGATIVITY

To Banish Bad Habits and Unpleasant Issues

(For best results, perform this spell on the Oak Moon. Good results can also be obtained during the Waning Moon.)

Materials

1 white candle
Several sprigs of holly

Place the holly around the base of the candle. Name the candle for any bad habits or unpleasant issues that have entered your life in the past year, then light it. Release the negativity by saying something like:

I release you, negativity
I release your hold on me
I banish you from mind and heart
And give myself a fresh new start
From this moment I am free
As I will so mote it be

When the candle burns all the way down, toss the holly in the hearth fire or burn it in a fireproof dish. Know that life has begun anew.

Mischief-Dispelling Fairy Garden

(For best results, perform this spell on the Hare Moon. Good results can also be obtained during the Waning Moon.)

Materials
13 dimes

Fairies are not always the fun-loving, gentle creatures we believe them to be. In fact, if left to their own devices they can create more mischief, mayhem, and negativity than you can shake a stick at. For that reason, leave a small area of your garden or flowerbed untended and offer it to the fairies, saying something like:

> *Fairies, gnomes, and other fey*
> *I offer you this spot today*
> *To tend however you see fit*
> *To build your homes with full permit*
> *To live and laugh, to work and play*
> *Provided there comes not a day*
> *When you bring mayhem unto me*
> *And if to this, you all agree*
> *I welcome you with warm embrace*
> *Come one and all to claim your space*

Scatter the dimes across the area and know that no mischief will ever come from the fairy folk.

OPPORTUNITY
Chant to Bring Personal Opportunity

(For best results, perform this chant on the Chaste Moon. Good results can also be obtained during the Waxing Moon.)

> *Maiden, now fling forth the doors*
> *And unblock all the corridors*
> *Clear all paths and avenues*
> *And open every window, too*
> *So opportunities flow free*
> *And make themselves known to me*
> *Help me to see every one*
> *As I will, so be it done*

PERSONAL GROWTH
Personal Growth Spell

(For best results, perform this spell on the Wort Moon. Good results can also be obtained during the Waxing Moon.)

Materials
Wildflower or herb seeds

Scatter the seeds outdoors while calling forth the Spirits of the Earth by saying something like:

> *Good Spirits of the Earth, I call*
> *Rise up—come forward one and all—*
> *Empower me now as I grow*
> *So as the winds of change do blow*
> *I stand firmly in my task*
> *And one more thing, too, that I ask*
> *Is that You ease the pain of growth*
> *And give to me a solid oath*
> *That You'll support me as I grow*
> *From bud to blossom in Life's flow*

As the seeds begin to grow, so will your strength to handle personal growth issues.

PETS

General Pet Blessing

(For best results, perform this spell on the Blood Moon. Good results can also be obtained during the Waxing Moon.)

Hold your pet and stroke him or her lovingly. If this isn't possible, as in the case of fish, put your hands on the containment area and spend a few minutes speaking to your pet. Once the energy is flowing well between you, bless your pet by saying something like:

> *I bless you in the Lady's Name*
> *Be kept from harm and loss and pain*
> *None but joy shall light each day*
> *As in the Lady's care you play*

PROBLEM SOLVING
Chant to the Mother for Quick Resolution

(For best results, perform this spell on the Mead/Honey Moon. Good results can also be obtained during the Waxing Moon.)

> *Mother Goddess, lift Your eyes*
> *And aid me now, for You are Wise*
> *Help me to look at every angle*
> *Of this situation, and untangle*
> *The threads just serving to deceive*
> *Shed Your light that I receive*
> *A good solution to this mess*
> *With speed and fairness, too, please bless*
> *Me as I work unto this task*
> *Mother, do now as I ask*

PRODUCTIVITY
Project Completion Charm

(For best results, perform this spell on the Snow Moon. Good results can also be obtained during the Waxing Moon.)

Materials
1 purple candle

To-do list

3 cloves of garlic

1 small piece of moonstone

1 small white or yellow charm bag

Light the candle and place the list in front of it. Visualize a purple aura enveloping the list and all the spell materials. When the color begins to deepen, place the garlic and moonstone inside the bag. Hold the bag between your eyebrows and chant something like:

> *Moonlike stone so white and round*
> *Bulbs that thrive beneath the ground*
> *Help me put this list to rest*
> *Without becoming tired or stressed*
> *Help me work through each assignment*
> *Without restriction or confinement*
> *Until each one is put to bed*
> *And no longer wanders through my head*

Place the bag on top of the list and leave it there. When the candle burns out, place the bag under your bed while you sleep. Work diligently on the list the next day.

PROPHETIC DREAMS
Dream Pillow

(For best results, perform this spell on the Snow Moon. Good results can also be obtained during the Waxing Moon.)

Materials

2 4-inch squares of fabric in your choice of color
   and pattern
Small amount of fiberfill

½ teaspoon each of three or four of the following:
    anise; chamomile; mugwort; rosemary; cloves;
    mint; lavender; poppy seed; rose petals
1 blue candle
Needle and thread

With right sides facing each, take ¼-inch seams and sew the square together on three sides to form a sack. Turn the sack inside out, stuff with a bit of fiberfill, and set aside.

Mix your choice of herbs together, chanting something like:

> *Herbs now mix and bring me visions*
> *From afar with these provisions:*
> *That I see just what I should*
> *That everything is understood*
> *And that my memory serves me well*
> *So when I wake, the memories gel*
> *Do now what I ask of thee*
> *As I will, so mote it be*

Place the herbs in the sack, then finish stuffing the pillow with fiberfill. Turn the open edges toward the inside, and stitch the pillow closed.

Light the candle and place the pillow in front of it. Visualize prophetic dreams filtering through while you sleep, then charge the pillow by saying something like:

> *O dreaming tool, I conjure you*
> *To do the job I ask of you*

> *Issue visions unto me*
> *As I will, so mote it be*

After the candle burns out, slip the pillow inside the pillowcase with your bed pillow and sleep on it nightly.

To Invoke Prophetic Dreams

(For best results, perform this spell on the Storm Moon. Good results can also be obtained during the Waxing Moon.)

Materials

1 small piece of amethyst

Use your dominant hand to hold the stone to the spot between your eyebrows. When the stone begins to pulse, enchant it by saying something like:

> *Purple stone of prophecy*
> *Bring future visions unto me*
> *Bring them while I'm fast asleep*
> *Through the dream world let them creep*
> *And so I recollect them all*
> *Grant good memory and recall*
> *Let them flow to me with ease*
> *O purple stone of prophecies*

Place the stone under your pillow.

PSYCHISM

Charm to Increase Psychism

(For best results, perform this spell on the Storm Moon. Good results can also be obtained during the Waxing Moon.)

Materials

1 purple candle

1 small piece of amethyst or sodalite

1 tablespoon mugwort

Small charm bag or white handkerchief

Place the charm bag in front of the candle and light the wick. Hold the stone in your dominant hand and wait until you can feel it pulse, then charge the stone by saying something like:

> *Stone exuding psychic power*
> *Become more potent with each hour*
> *And bring your psychic strengths to me*
> *Lending them that I might see*
> *What I should to help all those*
> *Who come to me with questions posed*
> *A psychic tool, become for me*
> *As I will, so mote it be*

Place the stone inside the bag or in the middle of the handkerchief, then sprinkle the mugwort on top, saying something like:

Herb revered for psychic speed
To the words I speak, now heed
Boost the power of this stone
So psychic skills are finely honed
And magnified within my core
So that they fill me evermore

Close the bag or tie the materials securely in the hand-kerchief, then put the parcel back in front of the candle and say:

Psychic tool of potency
Bring now what I ask of thee
Increase my skills and clarity
As I will, so mote it be

Leave the parcel in front of the candle until the wick burns out, then keep the bag with your divination tools or carry it on your person.

⭐ ———————————————————

Charge and wear a black opal to open the door to psychic communications and increase magical skill.

——————————————————— ⭐

RELATIONSHIPS

To Mend a Relationship

(For best results, perform this spell on the Wolf Moon. Good results can also be obtained during the Waning Moon.)

Visualize the person with whom you wish to mend the rift, then visualize a pink heart with the right-hand quarter removed. Once you have both images well-fixed in your mind's eye, superimpose the heart on the person's chest as you chant something like:

> *Remove the rift that plagues us now*
> *Cast it out and then allow*
> *(Name of person)'s heart to open wide*
> *And let me once again inside*
> *And once I have been let back in*
> *Never let us part again*

To Secure Family Harmony

(For best results, perform this spell on the Wolf Moon. Good results can also be obtained during the Waxing Moon.)

Materials

6 peeled apples cut crosswise into wedges

Cinnamon

Cookie sheets

Wire coat hanger

Pliers

Ribbon (optional)

Place the apple slices in a single layer on the cookie sheets, and sprinkle them heavily with cinnamon while chanting something like:

> *Fruit and spice, ye tools of love*
> *Let your essence surround us like a glove*
> *Binding us fast with laughter and care*
> *And real understanding in all that we share*
> *Keep our family secure now in true harmony*
> *As I do will it, now so shall it be*

Bake the slices in the oven at 150 degrees for two hours.

When the apples have cooled completely, cut the hook from the coat hanger and fashion a circle from the wire. String the slices onto the wire, then twist the ends together to close the wreath. Add a bow if you like, and hang in a prominent place in the home.

RELEASE

Spell to Release Useless Possessions or Ideas

(For best results, perform this spell on the Chaste Moon. Good results can also be obtained during the Waning Moon.)

Materials

1 white candle

Light the white candle in honor of the Chaste Moon. Then ask Her to help simplify your life by giving you the gumption to get rid of everything that's old and useless. Enlist Her aid by saying something like:

> *O wondrous Moon of pure, white light*
> *I ask Your help upon this night*
> *Help me to release all things*
> *To which, worn-out, I try to cling*
> *Old notions and ideas must go—*
> *As well as things that I well know*
> *Are useless—to accommodate a new*
> *And simpler life. I beg of You:*
> *Help me clear them all away*
> *And simplify my life today*

As the candle burns, sort through your material possessions and get rid of the things you no longer need. Know that by the time the candle burns out, the Chaste Moon will already have made great progress in clearing away any useless perceptions as well.

THANKSGIVING
To Honor the Earth

(For best results, perform this spell on the Wine/Harvest Moon. Good results can also be obtained during the Waxing Moon.)

Materials

1 piece of the season's best fruit

Wash the fruit thoroughly. If it's an apple or other fruit with a shiny surface, take care to polish the peel to a high gloss. Then take the fruit outside and give it back to Mother Earth by burying it in the ground. As you cover it, say something like:

> *I offer You, O Mother Earth*
> *This perfect fruit in love and mirth*
> *With many thanks for all You do*
> *A gift of love from me to You*

To Honor Sustenance Plants and Animals

(For best results, perform this spell on the Blood Moon. Good results can also be obtained during the Waxing Moon.)

Materials

1 red seven-day candle

Light the candle and place it on a windowsill. Ideally, the window should be facing West, but if that isn't possible, any windowsill will do. Raise your hands, palms up, and invite the spirits of the departed animals and plants by saying:

> *I invite you forth—now come to me—*
> *All giving their lives that I might be*
> *Nourished and satisfied, healthy and fit*

> *For it's in love that this candle is lit*
> *It serves as a symbol of the thanks that I give*
> *For the sacrifice made that all here might live*
> *So accept now this token of honor as you—*
> *Much honored guests—receive now your due*
> *And when you must go, I pray that you rest*
> *In the arms of the Lady until your next quest*

Let the candle burn all the way down.

WISHES

To Enlist the Aid of the Fey

(For best results, perform this spell on the Wort Moon. Good results can also be obtained during the Waxing Moon.)

Materials

A handful of chamomile

9 dimes

Toss a bit of chamomile into each corner of your yard, then strew the rest of the herb in the center, saying something like:

> *Fairies, gnomes, sprites, nymphs, and fey*
> *I ask your help upon this day*
> *Bring what I wish and bring it now*
> *And once I have it, this I vow:*
> *Nine shiny dimes I'll give to you*
> *In payment for the work you do*

> *But once you're paid, then you must go*
> *As I will, now be it so*

Once the fey deliver your wish, though, you must keep your promise to avoid any mayhem. Toss a dime in each corner of the yard, and place the rest in the middle.

Waning Moon Phase Efforts

ABUSE

Freedom from Abuse Spell

(Abuse of any kind is a serious matter. Please do whatever is necessary to stop it—phoning the police comes to mind here—before working this spell.)

Materials

> 1 black reversible candle with white center (you may also use a white candle completely colored with a black permanent marker)
> 1 small piece of black onyx

Light the candle and hold the stone in your dominant hand. See the stone growing larger until it forms a wall between you and the abusive person, completely separating you from the harm. Then evoke the power of the Waning Moon by saying something like:

> *As You decrease in size and light*
> *Waning Moon, please heed my plight*
> *Your disseminating power send*

> *To bring this harm unto an end*
> *Free me quickly—free me now*
> *And never once again allow*
> *Me to slip into this place*
> *Free me with Your fading face*

Leave the stone in front of the candle until the wick extinguishes itself, then carry the stone with you. Toss the stone into running water when you've been freed from the situation.

⭐ —————————————————————

Black tourmaline, when carried or worn, is an excellent preventative measure against future physical or mental abuse.

————————————————— ⭐

ADDICTION

Waning Moon Chant to Stop Cravings

(While this chant will work to curb minor cravings, please understand that it will not cure serious addictions on its own. For serious problems with addiction, use it during the Waning Moon along with the prescribed treatment of your health care practitioner.)

> *Waning Moon up in the sky*
> *Help me from your place on high*
> *Curb my cravings as Your light*
> *Fades to darkness in the night*

Decrease their power gradually
Until they have no hold on me
Waning Moon, I conjure Thee
As I will, so mote it be

To help curb addictive cravings, carry or wear a piece of hematite.

ANGER

Anger Relief Tea

Materials

1 small piece of amethyst

1 teabag (your choice of flavor and brand)

2 sprigs bruised, fresh mint, or ¼ teaspoon dried mint

1 cup boiling water

Paper coffee filter

String

Begin by tearing off a piece of coffee filter about three times as large as the stone. Wrap the stone inside, twist the top, secure with string, and set aside. Then add the tea and mint to the cup of water and watch the tea color the water for a few seconds. Breathe in the minty fragrance, saying something like:

Boiling water, flow throughout
This tea and herb to cast about

> *A spell of cooling, soothing mint*
> *To dispel anger and all hint*

Drop the amethyst "parcel" into the tea, then say:

> *Of aggravation, stress, and woe*
> *And all annoyances that slow*
> *My progress to a calm condition*
> *Tranquility is now your mission*

Allow the tea to steep for a few minutes, then say something like:

> *Tea of mint and cooling peace*
> *As I sip you, all shall cease*
> *But calm, clear thoughts within my head*
> *Erase all anger and its stead*
> *My sense of reason, too, return*
> *Please drown out fury's constant burn*
> *Till I am pure tranquility*
> *As I will, so mote it be*

Sip the tea and feel anger fly away.

ANXIETY
Panic Attack Relief Spell

Materials
1 white candle
1 small amount of dried thyme
Vegetable oil

Anoint the candle with oil, then roll it in the thyme. Light the candle and watch it burn for a few seconds, knowing that your anxiety is melting away with the candle wax. Smell the fragrance of the thyme filling the air, and feel the aroma transporting you to a calmer, happier place. Then say something like:

> *Anxiety, now melt away*
> *As wick and wax now do today*
> *And as you melt, so does your power*
> *Over me, it cannot tower*
> *Herb of thyme does its part, too*
> *By crushing all the life from you*
> *You are weak and you must flee*
> *As I will, so mote it be*

Let the candle burn out, and know that anxiety has died with the flame.

Carry a piece of amethyst with you to ease anxiety attacks. Rub it for a few seconds when you feel an attack coming on.

APATHY

Spell to Remove Apathy

Materials

1 orange candle

1 small piece of black tourmaline

Light the candle and watch as the wax begins to melt. Hold the stone in your dominant hand and chant something like:

> *Apathy, be gone from me*
> *You have no place that I can see*
> *Within my life or in my soul*
> *Your presence is a gaping hole*
> *That swallows up all that is good*
> *And keeps me from caring as I should*
> *About the things that really matter*
> *My hopes and dreams, you shred and shatter*
> *And so I cast you out today*
> *Go now! Flee! Be on your way!*
> *For once this Moon has turned to black*
> *You'll lose all power to attack*

Close your eyes and will all the indifference and lack of enthusiasm inside you to enter the stone. Place the stone in front of the candle and snuff out the wick.

Repeat the process until the first day of the Dark Moon, then let the candle burn all the way down. Toss the stone into running water.

AUTOMOBILES

Charm to Prevent Vehicle Malfunction

Materials

1 purple candle

1 small piece of lepidolite

1 small clear quartz crystal

1 small piece of orange calcite

1 three-leafed clover

¼ teaspoon cinnamon

⅛ teaspoon ginger

1 4-by-4-inch square of red fabric

Light the candle and visualize your vehicle working properly and being free from all malfunction. Place the fabric in front of the candle and put the lepidolite in the center with the other stones, one on each side. Hold your hands over the stones and say something like:

> *Powerful stones of perfect protection*
> *Bond now as one with seamless connection*
> *To guard well my vehicle from all duress*
> *And keep, too, at bay problematical stress*
> *So all parts work well and they all hold together*
> *Regardless of mileage or changes in weather*
> *Now with these words, your magic's set free*
> *By Waning Moon's power, as I will, it shall be*

Place the clover over the lepidolite and sprinkle the herbs on top, saying something like:

> *Herbs that protect from all sorts of malfunctions*
> *Work with these stones without any compunction*
> *To keep vehicular problems held well at bay*
> *During my travels at night or by day*
> *Now with these words, your magic's set free*
> *By Waning Moon's power, as I will, it shall be*

Tie the corners of the cloth together to secure the ingredients, then leave the pouch in front of the candle until the wick burns out. Place the pouch in the glove box of your vehicle.

BEAUTY
Purification Mask

Materials

1 container of your favorite peel-off mask

Two nights after the Full Moon, take the container to a window. Then, holding it in cupped hands with palms turned up, beseech the Waning Moon by saying something like:

> *Waning Moon of fading light*
> *Please work Your magic of the night*
> *Upon this substance for my face*
> *So blemishes it shall erase*
> *So imperfections fade with You*
> *And facial flaws leave quickly, too*
> *So all that there is left to see*
> *Is pure radiance. So mote it be.*

Leave the container on the windowsill overnight, then use the mask every Monday.

> If acne is a problem, rub a rose quartz on the affected areas once daily as you visualize the imperfections dissipating.

CLEANSING

To Cleanse Stones, Jewelry, and Small Altar Objects

Materials

Plastic zippered bags

Objects to be cleansed

Place your hands, palms down, over the objects and see current energies begin to lift and separate. Say something like:

> *Current ingrained energies*
> *I conjure you to change with ease*
> *In shape and form and neutralize*
> *Until I can reenergize*
> *You into that which works for me*
> *As I will, so mote it be*

Place the objects in the bags, zip them shut, and leave them in the freezer compartment of your refrigerator for twenty-four hours to eliminate old energies. Remove items from the freezer and charge for whatever you like.

COMMUNICATION
Bath to Eradicate Timidity

Materials

Handful of table salt

1 black onyx

Toss the salt and stone into your bath water while chanting something like:

> *Wash all mental blocks away*
> *Within this stone now, they must stay*
> *As well as negativity*
> *And all that has a hold on me*
> *So that my thoughts flow clear and free*
> *And issue forth effectively*

Completely immerse yourself in the bath nine times, while visualizing all shyness being washed away. Allow your body to dry naturally, then bury the stone or release it into a body of water.

COOPERATION

Dissension Removal Spell

Materials

1 mauve or orange candle

Vegetable oil

Cinnamon

Allspice

Clove

Inscribe the candle with a spider web to symbolize the group in question and their connections to each other, then draw a pentagram on top of the web. Anoint the candle with vegetable oil while visualizing everyone cooperating with each other and handling their workloads pleasantly and efficiently. Roll the candle in the herbs. Light the candle and chant:

> *By ancient art of flame and wax*
> *And herb and rhyme that counteracts:*
> *Dissension flees as candle shrinks*
> *Strengthening connecting links*
> *So all will help and work as one*
> *Until all tasks are finally done.*
> *Cooperation is my plea*
> *As I will, so mote it be*

Allow the candle to burn down completely.

DEPRESSION
Depression Relief Spell

Materials

1 black or navy blue candle

Paper and pen

Fireproof dish

Using the pen, inscribe the candle with the word "depression," then make a list of all the things you're upset and depressed about. It's important to be brutally honest here, so don't leave anything out, even if you think it's silly. Once you've finished, light the candle and place the list in front of it.

Visualize yourself plucking each item on the list from your life, and totally destroying it. Handle these one by one until you can see that they all cease to live, then say something like:

> *Depression, that which causes doubt*
> *From my heart, I cast you out*
> *I am strong and you are weak*
> *Havoc you no longer wreak*
> *As I pluck you from my life*
> *I melt away all pain and strife*

Place the list in the fireproof dish, then set the list on fire, saying something like:

> *There is no room for compromise*
> *Burn to ash before my eyes*

> *And with you dies your hold on me*
> *As I will, so mote it be*

After the ashes cool, flush them down the toilet.

DIETING

Blue Topaz Dieting Spell

Materials

1 black candle

1 blue topaz jewelry item or a small piece of the stone

Pencil

Using the pencil, inscribe the word "fat" on the candle. Light the candle and visualize any excess fat beginning to melt away as the candle burns. Place the stone or jewelry in front of the candle, cover it with your dominant hand, and say something like:

> *I conjure you unto this task*
> *A loss of pounds is what I ask*
> *Hold overeating well at bay*
> *Keep harmful urges far away*
> *To food consumption, bring control*
> *Until I reach my dieting goal*
> *Force excess fat to dissipate*
> *To bring me to a healthy weight*
> *And return my physical energy*
> *As I will, so mote it be*

Leave the item in front of the candle until the wick burns out, then carry the stone or wear the jewelry while you're dieting.

For additional help in fighting cravings for sweets and fatty foods, use the Waning Moon Chant found under "Addiction."

ENEMIES

Enemy Attitude-Changing Spell

Materials

1 pink or peach candle

1 wooden craft stick

1 quart jar with a screw-on lid

1 cup sugar

Indelible marking pen

Light the candle and see your enemy's attitude toward you changing. See the person as being cordial and friendly, then write his or her name on the stick and carefully pass it through the candle flame while saying something like:

By firelight

Blow on the stick and say:

And gentle breeze

Hold the stick with a hand on each end and say:

> *By wood of Earth*

Lick your index finger and slide it down the length of the stick, over the name, and say:

> *And sparkling seas*

Place the stick in the jar and say something like:

> *I displace your attitude*
> *So you can't sulk or scheme or brood*
> *Or bring me harm in any way*
> *I steal its power now, today*

Pour the sugar on top of the stick and say something like:

> *By sugar, sweet, I rearrange*
> *Your feelings toward me and they change*
> *To sweetest thoughts that are infused*
> *With kindness that is so profuse*
> *You can't resist the urge to be*
> *More than pleasant unto me*

Pour water into the jar until it is about one inch from the top, and say something like:

> *By flow of Water, magic's free*
> *It goes to work immediately*

Screw the top on tightly, then shake the jar to dissolve the sugar while saying something like:

And as I mix this syrup, sweet
You come to know that you must treat
Me with respect and courtesy
As I will, so mote it be

Keep the jar safe in a dark place (cabinets and closets work well for this).

FEAR

Waning Moon Novena to Alleviate Fear

Materials

1 black reversible candle with white center (you may
   use a white candle completely colored with
   a black permanent marker)

Begin three days after the Full Moon by lighting the candle. See all fears evaporate, and visualize yourself as being happy, healthy, and unafraid. Then say something like:

Fear, release your hold on me
Your power lacks the energy
To hold me as it did before
You've lost your grasp upon my core
You've lost the force that you once had
To terrify or drive me mad
The battle's over—I have won—
My angst is gone and you are done
For as the Moon wanes in the sky
You wilt and wither, fall and die

Let the candle burn for about five minutes, then snuff the flame. Repeat the spell every day until the Moon is dark. Let the candle burn all the way down on the last day.

FRIENDSHIP

Spell to Remove Loneliness

Materials

1 black or dark gray candle

1 3-inch square of black knitted or crocheted fabric
   (a piece cut from an old sweater or sock works
   well for this)

A piece of white chalk (optional)

Begin by naming the candle and the fabric for loneliness; in fact, you may inscribe that word on both if you like (use the chalk for the fabric). Light the candle and see your loneliness and isolation melting away with the wax. Sit in front of the candle and begin to unravel the fabric while saying something like:

> *Loneliness I now unravel*
> *As my fingers quickly travel*
> *What once trapped me I now loose*
> *As a measure to induce*
> *Friendship to come forth to me*
> *With love and fun and pleasantry*
> *Loneliness, I steal your power*
> *Flee from me this very hour*

Continue to chant until the fabric is completely unraveled, then wrap the thread around your hand to form a coil. Slip the coil from your hand and tie a knot in the center to represent the new circle of friends you desire. Say something like:

> *I now transform you into friends*
> *And others whom I invite in*

Leave the knotted thread in front of the candle until the wick extinguishes itself, then carry the bundle of thread with you.

GOSSIP

Spell to Stop Gossip

Materials

1 white figure candle in the proper gender
A pinch of slippery elm
1 1-by-6-inch strip of black cloth
1 yard of string, yarn, or twine
Sharp knife (a craft knife works well)
A match

Hollow out the mouth area of the candle and then soften the wax with a lit match. Press the slippery elm into the space and say something like:

> *No more ill of me you speak*
> *For herbs now make your tongue so weak*

> *That only pleasantries can come*
> *From your mouth and wagging tongue*

Fold the cloth in half lengthwise, then tie it over the herbs and around the mouth of the figure candle like a gag. Secure the gag with a knot, saying something like:

> *But should you think to speak some ill*
> *This gag prevents it as I will*

Fold the string in half to find the center point. Then, placing that point behind the feet, wrap the candle up and down in a crisscrossing motion until it is wrapped foot to head and back down again. Tie it securely, and then say something like:

> *You have no power over me*
> *I've tied you up and I am free*
> *You cannot work toward my disgrace*
> *While in this rope you are encased*
> *And so you shall forever stay*
> *Though free to move and work and play*

Place the figure in a corner of the room, facing outward, and leave it there. Should you need to move it to a new location, slide a file folder behind the figure to keep its back in a corner, and pack it carefully in a box with plenty of stuffing so the herbs won't be dislodged.

HABITS

Spell to Relieve Bad Habits

Materials
1 black candle
⅛ teaspoon ginger
Vegetable oil
Paper and pen
Permanent black marker
Fireproof dish

Anoint the candle with oil and roll it in the ginger, then light the candle and list all of your bad habits on the paper. If you like, increase the list by adding any unsavory characteristics you'd like to alleviate as well. Once you're finished, use the marker to draw a big black *X* through everything on your list. Then muster up an attitude and throw the paper to the floor, stomping it with your feet, and screaming something like:

> *I stomp on you, you're hurt and weak,*
> *Your power's gone, your future's bleak*

Pick up the paper and tear it to bits while yelling something like:

> *I tear you up, you cannot live*
> *No more grief to me you'll give*

Dump the pieces of paper in the fireproof dish and laugh out loud at them. Then set them on fire, saying something like:

> *By flame of fire I take your life*
> *In ash you cannot cause me strife*

Finally, toss the ashes in the toilet and flush them down, saying:

> *And now into the sewer I throw*
> *These things that used to cause me woe*
> *I've flushed them from my life today*
> *And away from me, they must now stay*

Let the candle burn out and know that these troubles are now history.

HEALTH/HEALING

Healing Spell

Materials

1 pale blue candle

Pencil

Inscribe the candle with your health problem, then superimpose a "7" on top, the lower leg of which corkscrews from right to left to make three complete loops. Light the candle and visualize the affected area as bright red. Holding the image in your mind's eye, mentally paint the area a soft, cool, healing green. Then say something like:

> *Symbol that can cure all ills*
> *And healing green, bend to my will*
> *Eradicate the problem here*

> *Cast off damage, cast out fear,*
> *And bring good health at once to me*
> *As I will, so mote it be*

Let the candle burn all the way down, and continue any medications prescribed by your healthcare practitioner.

HEARTBREAK

Spell to Ease a Broken Heart

Go outside, raise your arms to the sky, and summon the Winds, saying something like:

> *I conjure You, O Mighty Winds*
> *To put this pain now to an end*

Turn to the East and say:

> *East Wind, lend your consolation*
> *Blow away my desolation*

Moving in a counterclockwise motion, turn to the North and say:

> *North Wind, blow with galelike force*
> *To rip pain from its very source*

Turn to the West and say:

> *West Wind, with Your cleansing power*
> *Sweep away all that is sour*

Turn to the South and say:

> *And South Wind, with Your warm embrace*
> *Kiss me gently on the face*
> *And bring joy back into my heart*
> *Giving me a brand new start*

Finally, return to the center and say:

> *O Mighty Winds, I summon You*
> *Cleanse this painful residue*
> *Come forth now, I conjure Thee*
> *To take this heartbreak far from me*

Turn and walk away without looking back. Know that the Winds will do Their jobs.

HOME

Home Purification

Materials

1 stick or cone for each room of either frankincense
    or dragon's blood incense
1 small bowl of water
Table salt

Put the incense in holders or fireproof dishes, and place one in the center of each room. Add nine tablespoons of salt to the water, then take the bowl and go to the room in the eastern-most portion of the home. Light the incense in that room. Next, with bowl in hand, move to the eastern wall. Moving clockwise and using your fingers, sprinkle the baseboards with the saltwater while saying something like:

All malevolence now must die
By Fire and Water, Earth and Sky
Negativity, too, must flee
By Air and Fire and Earth and Sea
Only joy may cross these lines
The rest is banished for all time
I cleanse you of old energies
As I will, so mote it be

When you reach the North and complete the circle, move clockwise until you reach the door. Proceed to the next room and continue to repeat the process until all rooms are cleansed.

To Seal or Ward Portals in the Home

Materials

½ lemon for each drain and toilet in the home

Cut the lemons in half, crosswise. Squeeze the juice of each piece down a drain or toilet while saying something like:

By the juice of fruit ruled by the Sun
Return at once from whence you've come
I banish you and seal this place
From your invasion to my space
Your spirit's blocked eternally
As I will, so mote it be

When you're finished, wet your fingers with the pulp and use them to draw a tiny banishing pentagram on the tops and bottoms of each window frame while saying the same words.

INCENSE

Waning/Dark Moon Incense

Materials

⅛ teaspoon anise

1 teaspoon lavender

1 teaspoon wormwood or patchouli

Pinch of camphor

Charcoal block

Mix the herbs well during the Waning Moon, then charge the incense by saying something like:

> *As Moon decreases in the night*
> *I free your power to take flight*
> *And bring the things I ask of thee*
> *As I will, so mote it be*

Burn on a charcoal block.

JUSTICE
Spell for Swift Justice

Materials

1 yellow candle

1 orange candle

Light the candles and see the scales of justice tipping in your favor, then beseech the Crone and the Deities of Justice to come to your aid by saying the following prayer:

> *O Wisest Crone, I call to You*
> *All Deities of Justice, I call You, too*
> *Work together in this task*
> *And bring to me just what I ask:*
> *Wield the justice I deserve*
> *Hold nothing back in Your reserve*
> *Work Your magic now for me*
> *As I will, so mote it be*

Blow out the candles and repeat this spell every day for the next eight days, letting the candles burn all the way down on the last day. Know that justice will be served and all parties will get exactly what's coming to them.

LIBERATION

Spell to Break Free of That Which Holds You Back

Materials

1 small wooden stick (or use a craft stick
if you like)

Hold the stick in both hands and visualize it as being the central part of a fence that keeps you from your goals—a fence so high and sturdy that there's no way to get over or under it. Holding the image in your mind's eye, scream at the top of your lungs:

> *Loosen up now, bonds that hold*
> *Weaken as the Moon grows old*
> *Until your power's gone for good*
> *And snaps apart like splintered wood*
> *Waning Moon, now work for me*
> *Break these bonds and set me free*

Break the stick into pieces (as many as you can) and scatter them on the winds. Know that all restrictions will fade as the Moon wanes.

★ ——————————————————
Carrying or wearing a sprig of mistletoe imparts freedom of mind and encourages the bearer to make independent decisions.
—————————————————— ★

LOVE

To Reverse a Love Spell

Materials

1 drop lemon juice

1 reversible candle (black outer with red center),
　　or 1 red candle (color the outside with a black
　　permanent marker)

Drop the lemon juice on the candle wick and wait for it
to dry. Then inscribe the name of the person from whom
you wish to remove the spell on the candle (anywhere
will do). Light the candle and see the person being free
from all bewitchments. Holding the image firmly in your
mind's eye, say something like:

> *Reverse now colors of this wax*
> *Free (name of person) of the bounds that*
> *Held her (him) fast*
> *By flaming wick and cleansing juice*
> *I demand you cut (name of person) loose*
> *I break the spell that held her (him) tight*
> *She's (he's) free to let new love take flight*

Let the candle burn down completely, then dispose of
any leftover wax in running water. If there is a minimal
amount, just flush it down the toilet.

LUCK

Chant to Break a Run of Bad Luck

Winds of Change, now hear my plea
Blow misfortune far from me
Fires of Sun and golden flash
Burn misfortune now to ash
Cleansing Waters, flow this day
And wash misfortune clean away
Solid Earth, on You, I call
To bar misfortune with Your wall
So that it cannot crawl or creep
Or reach for me while I'm asleep
From misfortune, set me free
As I will, so mote it be

MEDITATION

Premeditation Prayer to the Dark Maiden

Maiden of the Waning Moon
With my mind, please now attune
And cast off trivialities
So I can meditate with ease
And hear the answers as they flow
And understand what I should know
Darkest Maiden, hear my plea
As I will, so mote it be

MONEY
Debt-Banishing Spell

Materials

1 black candle

Fireproof dish

Paper and pen

List your debts and their amounts on a piece of paper, then inscribe the total amount on the candle. Fold the paper five times and place it in front of the candle. Light the candle and visualize yourself being free from financial worry, and all your debts being resolved. Then chant something like:

> *Sun and Air and Earth and Sea*
> *Take these debts away from me*
> *Remove the blockage high and low*
> *So I can pay just what I owe*
> *Financial freedom's what I ask*
> *I conjure Thee unto this task*

Light the paper from the candle flame and burn it to ash in the fireproof dish. When the candle burns completely down, bury the ashes from the paper outdoors.

NIGHTMARES
Stone Charm to Dispel Nightmares

Materials

1 small piece of citrine

With your dominant hand, hold the stone to the spot between your eyebrows. When the stone begins to pulse, enchant it by saying something like:

> *Stone of peaceful, dreaming sleep*
> *Let no nightmares this way creep*
> *Keep all terrors far away*
> *Hold unpleasantness at bay*
> *So happy dreams are all I see*
> *Do now what I ask of thee*

Keep the stone under your pillow while you sleep.

OBSTACLES

Spell to Remove Obstacles

Materials
1 green candle
Dried rosemary
Vegetable oil

Inscribe the candle with your obstacles, then anoint it with oil and roll it in the rosemary. Light the candle and see all obstacles melting away with the candle. Then say something like:

> *Herb and wax, now melt away*
> *And as you do upon this day*
> *Melt obstacles away as well—*
> *Every solitary cell—*
> *So paths are clear and I may pass*

And move along about my tasks
Herb and wax, I conjure thee
Melt obstacles away for me

Let the candle burn out.

PEACE
Spell for a Peaceful Mind

Materials

1 pale blue candle

¼ teaspoon each thyme, lemon balm, and lavender

1 small piece of black tourmaline

1 4-by-4-inch square of pale blue fabric

1 12-inch length of pale blue ribbon or yarn

Light the candle and visualize the frantic activity in your mind slowing down enough for you to rest and relax. Place the fabric in front of the candle, and sprinkle the herbs on top, saying something like:

Herbal mixture of tranquility
I conjure you to mesh and be
The force commanding wheels to slow
Within my head and drain the flow
Of worries with which I'm obsessed
And extraneous thoughts so I can rest
And bring your calming peace to me
As I will, so mote it be

Place the stone on top of the herbs and say something like:

> *Tourmaline, O blackest stone*
> *Work the magic of the Crone*
> *And with these herbs, I ask of you*
> *To bring the calmness I pursue*
> *Bring rest to mind and peace to core*
> *Absorbing idle thoughts before*
> *They take on life and can roam free*
> *Do now what I ask of thee*

Gather the edges of the fabric together and secure with the ribbon. Leave the pouch in front of the candle until the wick burns out, then hold the pouch to your forehead whenever confusion clouds your mind.

PEACEFUL SEPARATION

To Separate Oneself from a Bad Habit or Another Person

Materials

1 black candle

1 small piece black onyx

Light the candle and hold the stone in front of it. Visualize a wide space forming between you and the person or the bad habit, and see all related problems coming to an end. When the image is firmly fixed in your mind's eye, charge the stone, saying something like:

> *Stone of darkest coloration*
> *I conjure you with separation*
> *Bring space between us with this spell*
> *And with your power let it swell*
> *Till all related problems cease*
> *And at last, I'm left in peace*
> *Heed now, stone, this affirmation*
> *And bring a speedy separation*

Leave the stone in front of the candle until the wick burns out, then carry the stone with you.

PSYCHISM
Empathetic Shield Charm

Materials

1 small piece of black tourmaline

Hold the stone between your eyebrows and visualize it forming a shield so strong that the feelings, reactions, and emotional responses of other people cannot enter. Instead of seeing these responses bouncing off, though, see the stone absorbing them before they can seep inside. Then charge the stone by saying something like:

> *Striated stone of deepest black*
> *Absorb all thoughts that may attack*
> *So they can't seep into my head*
> *And fill me with their pain and dread*
> *Be ye now a shield of strength*
> *I conjure you for my life's length*

> *So all I feel belongs to me*
> *As I will, so mote it be*

Carry the stone with you constantly to keep from picking up on the thought patterns and emotional responses of those with whom you come in contact. Clear the stone of other people's energies at the end of each day by leaving it in the freezing compartment of your refrigerator overnight.

STRESS

Stress Relief Spell

Materials

1 sheet of white paper
Brightly colored crayons
Wide-tipped black permanent marker
Matches or cigarette lighter
Fireproof dish

Place the sheet of paper on a hard surface in front of you and begin to scribble on the paper with a crayon. Bold and erratic strokes are key here, because the art you're creating is a symbol of the stress you feel inside. Choose another color and work with it as you say something like:

> *A war against all stress I wage*
> *As I place it on this page*
> *And once it's transferred to this sheet*
> *Stress will meet with sure defeat*

Continuing to chant, choose another color, then another, and another, until the entire sheet is covered with bright, bold crayon marks.

When you're satisfied with the page, use the marker to draw an X from corner to corner, and say something like:

> *By the power of this X*
> *I cancel stress and its effects*
> *It's lost all power over me*
> *As I will, so mote it be*

Rip the paper to shreds and set them on fire in the dish. As it burns to ash, say something like:

> *All residue is now consumed*
> *So stress can never be exhumed*
> *By flame and smoke and ash, I'm free*
> *As I will, so mote it be*

When the ashes are cool, scatter them outdoors on the winds.

THEFT

Theft Prevention Spell

Materials

1–2 boxes of table salt

Patchouli oil

Begin by sprinkling the salt around the inner edges of each room in your home as well as the entrance thresholds, while saying something like:

Evil cannot cross this line
Regardless of its place in time
Thieves stay out and foes be gone
You may not cross the lines I've drawn

Then dip your index finger in the oil and mark a pentagram on each window screen and on the outside doorknobs, saying:

With patchouli oil, I seal
This home, removing all appeal
To thieves and those who wish us harm
And by the power of this charm
They are banished from this home
And cannot through its boundaries roam
Of them now this place is free
As I will so mote it be

Repeat as necessary every three months.

To further protect against theft, always keep a piece of garnet in the central room of your home.

TRAFFIC

Chant to Relieve Traffic Jams

(While inserted here for ease of placement, this chant may be used at any time, regardless of Moon phase.)

Traffic jam upon this road
Dissipate, decrease, erode
Until these cars again flow free
As I will, so mote it be

Appendix A

Magical Herb Use and Substitutions List

Anger Management: almond, catnip, chamomile, elecampane, lemon balm, lavender, mint, passion flower, rose, vervain

Anxiety Management: skullcap, valerian

Apathy: ginger, peppermint

Beauty: avocado, catnip, flax, ginseng, maidenhair fern, rosemary, witch hazel

Business Success: basil, frankincense, hawthorn, sandalwood, squill root

Courage: borage, cedar, columbine, masterwort, mullein, sweetpea, thyme, tonka bean, yarrow

Depression Management: camphor, catnip, celandine, daisy, dandelion, goldenrod, ground ivy, hawthorn, hazelnut, henbane, hibiscus, honeysuckle, hyacinth, lemon balm, lily of the valley, marjoram, meadowsweet, mugwort, pomegranate, saffron, shepherd's purse

Employment: bergamot, bayberry, bay leaf, pecan, pine

Enemies: patchouli, slippery elm

Friendship: lemon, orange, sunflower, sweetpea, tonka bean, vanilla

Gambling: buckeye, chamomile, pine

Health/Healing: allspice, apple, barley, bay leaf, blackberry, cedar, cinnamon, comfrey, elder, eucalyptus, fennel, flax, garlic, ginseng, golden seal, heliotrope, hops, horehound, ivy, lemon balm, life everlasting, mint, mugwort, myrrh, nasturtium, nutmeg, oak, olive, onion, peppermint, persimmon, pine, plantain, rosemary, rowan, rue, saffron, sandalwood, shepherd's purse, thistle, thyme, vervain, violet, willow, wintergreen, yerba santa

Heartbreak Management: apple, bittersweet, cyclamen, honeysuckle, jasmine, lemon balm, magnolia, peach, strawberry, yarrow

Legal Matters: buckthorn, celandine, chamomile, galangal, hickory, High John, marigold

Liberation: chicory, cypress, lavender, lotus, mistletoe, moonflower

Love: Adam-and-Eve root, allspice, apple, apricot, balm of Gilead, basil, bleeding heart, cardamom, catnip, chamomile, cinnamon, clove, columbine, copal, coriander, crocus, cubeb, daffodil, daisy, damiana, dill, elecampane, elm, endive, fig, gardenia, geranium, ginger, ginseng, hibiscus, hyacinth, indian paintbrush, jasmine, juniper, kava-kava, lady's mantle, lavender, lemon balm, lemon verbena, linden, lobelia, lotus, loveage, maidenhair fern, mandrake, maple, marjoram, myrtle, nutmeg, orchid, pansy, peach, peppermint, periwinkle, poppy, primrose, rose, rosemary, rue, saffron, skullcap, spearmint, spiderwort, strawberry, thyme, tonka bean, tulip, vanilla, vervain, violet, willow, wood betony, yarrow

Luck: allspice, anise, bluebell, calamus, china berry, daffodil, hazel, heather, holly, job's tears, linden, lucky hand, nutmeg, oak, orange, persimmon, pomegranate, poppy, rose, snakeroot, vetivert, violet

Lust: allspice, caraway, carrot, cattail, cinnamon, cinquefoil, clove, damiana, deerstongue, dill, foxglove, galangal, ginseng, hibiscus, mistletoe, parsley, rosemary, sesame, southernwood, vanilla, violet, yohimbe

Mental Powers: all heal, bay leaf, caraway, celery seed, forget-me-not, hazel, horehound, lily of the valley, lotus, pansy, periwinkle, rue, sandalwood, spikenard, summer savory, spearmint

Nightmare Prevention: chamomile, mullein

Prophetic Dreams: anise, chamomile, cinquefoil, cloves, heliotrope, jasmine, mimosa, mint, mugwort, rose, rosemary, valerian

Prosperity: bay leaf, basil, bergamot, cedar, chamomile, cinnamon, cinquefoil, clover, mandrake, marjoram, may apple, myrtle, oak, orange mint, parsley, pecan, pine, snapdragon, sunflower, sweet woodruff, tonka bean, tulip, vanilla, vervain, wheat

Protection: african violet, agrimony, aloe vera, alyssum, angelica, anise, arrowroot, asafetida, balm of Gilead, basil, bay leaf, birch, bladderwrack, boneset, bromeliad, broom, burdock, cactus, calamus, caraway, carnation, cedar, chrysanthemum, cinnamon, cinquefoil, clove, clover, cumin, curry, cyclamen, cypress, datura, dill, dogwood, dragon's blood, elder, elecampane, eucalyptus, fennel, feverwort, flax, fleabane, foxglove, frankincense, galangal, garlic, geranium, ginseng, heather, holly, honeysuckle, horehound, houseleek, hyacinth, hyssop, ivy, juniper, lady's slipper, larkspur, lavender, lilac, lily, linden, lotus, lucky hand, mallow, mandrake, marigold, mimosa, mint, mistletoe, mugwort, mulberry, mullein, mustard, myrrh, nettle, oak, olive, onion, parsley, pennyroyal, peony, pepper, periwinkle, pine, plantain, primrose, quince, radish, raspberry, rattlesnake root, rhubarb, rose, rowan, rue, sage, St. John's wort, sandalwood, snapdragon, southernwood, sweet woodruff, thistle, tulip, valerian, vervain, violet, willow, wintergreen, witch hazel, wolfbane, wormwood, wood betony, yucca

Psychic Ability: celery, cinnamon, citronella, elecampane, eyebright, flax, galangal, honeysuckle, lemongrass, mace, marigold, mugwort, peppermint, rose, rowan, star anise, thyme, uva ursa, wormwood, yarrow

Sleep: agrimony, chamomile, cinquefoil, elder, hops, lavender, linden, peppermint, rosemary, shepherd's purse, thyme, valerian, vervain

Strength: acorn, bay leaf, carnation, mugwort, mulberry, pennyroyal, plantain, St. John's wort, thistle

Stress Management: calendula, chamomile, comfrey, hops, lavender, nettle, oats, passion flower, St. John's wort, skullcap

Success: cinnamon, clover, ginger, High John, lemon balm, orange, rowan

Theft Prevention: caraway, elder, garlic, gentian, juniper, rosemary, vetivert

Travel: bladderwrack, lavender

Victory: bay leaf, High John, olive

Wisdom: hazel, rowan, sage, spikenard

Wishes: bay leaf, dandelion, dogwood, hazel, Job's tears, sage, sunflower, tonka bean, vanilla, vervain, violet, walnut

Appendix B

Magical Stone Use and Substitutions List

Anger Management: amethyst, carnelian, lepidolite, topaz

Beauty: amber, cat's-eye, jasper, opal, rose quartz, unakite

Business Success: green agate, aventurine, bloodstone, emerald, jade, lapis lazuli, malachite, green tourmaline

Change: ametrine, opal, unakite, watermelon tourmaline

Childbirth: geode, moonstone, mother-of-pearl

Courage: agate, amethyst, aquamarine, bloodstone, carnelian, diamond, hematite, lapis lazuli, tiger-eye, watermelon tourmaline, turquoise

Creativity: orange calcite, citrine, opal, topaz

Depression Management: blue agate, kunzite

Dieting: moonstone, blue topaz

Divination: amethyst, hematite, moonstone, opal, quartz crystal, rainbow obsidian, sodalite

Dreams: amethyst, azurite, citrine, opal, snowflake obsidian

Eloquence: carnelian, celestite, emerald

Friendship: chrysoprase, rose quartz, pink tourmaline, turquoise, amazonite, aventurine, tiger-eye

Gardening: green agate, moss agate, jade, malachite, quartz crystal

Bad Habit Management: moonstone, obsidian, black onyx

Healing/Health: green agate, banded agate, amethyst, aventurine, azurite, bloodstone, carnelian, chrysoprase, coral, diamond, peridot, petrified wood, quartz crystal, smoky quartz, sapphire, staurolite, sugilite, sunstone, yellow topaz, turquoise

Love: alexandrite, amber, amethyst, chrysocolla, diamond, emerald, jade, lapis lazuli, lepidolite, malachite, moonstone, opal, pearl, rose quartz, rhodocrosite, ruby, sapphire, topaz, pink tourmaline, turquoise

Luck: alexandrite, amber, apache tear, aventurine, chalcedony, chrysoprase, holey stones, lepidolite, opal, pearl, tiger-eye, turquoise

Lust: carnelian, coral, sunstone, mahogany obsidian

Magical Power: bloodstone, holey stones, quartz crystal, malachite, opal, ruby

Mental Ability: aventurine, citrine, emerald, fluorite, quartz crystal

Nightmare Prevention: chalcedony, citrine, holey stones, lepidolite, ruby

Peaceful Separation: black onyx, black tourmaline

Physical Energy: banded agate, garnet, quartz crystal, rhodocrosite, sunstone, tiger-eye

Prosperity: abalone, green agate, aventurine, bloodstone, chrysoprase, emerald, green tourmaline, jade, mother-of-pearl, malachite, opal, pearl, peridot, ruby, sapphire, staurolite, tiger-eye

Protection: apache tear, carnelian, chalcedony, chrysoprase, citrine, coral, diamond, emerald, flint, garnet, holey stones, jade, jasper, lapis lazuli, lepidolite, malachite, marble, moonstone, mother-of-pearl, obsidian, pearl, peridot, petrified wood, quartz crystal, ruby, salt, staurolite, sunstone, tiger-eye, smoky topaz, black tourmaline, turquoise

Psychic Ability: amethyst, aquamarine, azurite, citrine, emerald, holey stones, lapis lazuli, quartz crystal, sodalite, sugilite

Psychic Attack Management: alexandrite, fluorite, hematite, opal

Stress Management: amethyst, chrysoprase, leopard skin agate, jade, brecciated jasper, paua shell

Success: amazonite, chrysoprase, marble, sunstone

Theft Management: garnet, cubic zirconia

Travel: amethyst, aquamarine, chalcedony

Wisdom: amethyst, chrysocolla, coral, jade, sodalite, sugilite

Appendix C

Magical Candle Use and Substitutions List

Black: banishment, break bad habits, Crone aspect of the Triple Goddess, stop gossip, separation, uncovering truth, wisdom

Pale Blue: calmness, clarity, healing, peace, pleasant dreams, tranquility

Dark Blue: feminine deities, organization, water element

Brown: grounding, diffusing potentially harmful situations, relieve excess energy

Gold: financial increase, personal security, solar deities, the God

Green: Earth Element, fertility, growth, healing, independence, obstacle removal, productivity, prosperity

Lavender: stress and tension relief, knowledge retention, inner beauty, mental ability

Mauve: cooperation, intuitive power, psychic ability, self-confidence, self trust

Orange: attraction, business projects, business proposals, indifference, personal motivation, productivity, study

Peach: empathy, friendship, kindness, sympathy

Pink: friendship, harmony, love, romance, self-love

Purple: Akasha Element, job interviews, mental power, psychic power, protection, respect, spirituality, victory

Red: control, Fire Element, lust, Mother aspect of the Triple Goddess, passion, physical energy, physical strength, sexual desire, timidity relief

Silver: lunar deities, peace, serenity, the Goddess

Teal: agricultural efforts, balance, self-control, decision-making, practical matters, trust

Turquoise: diplomacy, eloquence, knowledge retention, logic, love, relaxation, stress relief, study

White: clarity, focus, Maiden aspect of the Triple Goddess, protection, substitution for any other color, spiritual guidance, tension relief

Yellow: Air Element, communication, creative endeavors, joy, success

Appendix D

Magical Associations of the Days of the Week

Sunday: business ventures and partnerships, work promotions, general and professional success, friendships, mental and physical health, joy

Monday: home and hearth, family, gardening, medicine, psychic development, prophetic dreaming, feminine issues

Tuesday: conflict, physical endurance and strength, lust, hunting, sports, competition, surgical procedures, political ventures, masculine issues

Wednesday: communication, inspiration and creativity, writers, poets, anything involving the written and spoken word, study, learning, teaching, self-improvement, self-understanding

Thursday: material gain, financial prosperity, gambling, good fortune, general success, accomplishment, honors and awards, legal issues

Friday: comfort, pleasure, and luxury, artistic endeavors, aromatherapy, love, romance, lust

Saturday: karmic issues, reincarnation, mysteries, wisdom, elderly people, death, the eradication of pests and disease

Appendix D

Magical Associations of the Days of the Week

Bibliography

Beyerl, Paul. *Master Book of Herbalism.* Custer, Wash.: Phoenix Publishing, 1984.

Brueton, Diana. *Many Moons.* New York: Prentice Hall Press, 1991.

Buckland, Raymond. *Buckland's Complete Book of Witchcraft.* St. Paul, Minn.: Llewellyn Publications, 1986.

Budapest, Zsuzsanna E. *Grandmother Moon.* New York: HarperSanFrancisco, 1991.

———. *The Grandmother of Time.* New York: HarperSanFrancisco, 1989.

Conway, D. J. *Moon Magick.* St. Paul, Minn.: Llewellyn Publications, 2000.

Cranmer, Thomas. *English Book of Common Prayer.* N.p., n.d.

Cunningham, Scott. *Cunningham's Encyclopedia of Crystal, Gem and Metal Magic.* St. Paul, Minn.: Llewellyn Publications, 1987.

———. *Cunningham's Encyclopedia of Magical Herbs.* St. Paul, Minn.: Llewellyn Publications, 1986.

———. *The Complete Book of Oils, Incenses, and Brews.* St. Paul, Minn.: Llewellyn Publications, 1989.

David, Judithann H., Ph.D. *Michael's Gemstone Dictionary.* Channeled by J. P. Van Hulle. Orinda, Calif.: The Michael Educational Foundation and Affinity Press, 1986.

Drew, A. J. *Wicca For Men.* Secaucus, N.J.: Carol Publishing Group, 1998.

Elias, Jason, and Katherine Ketcham. *In the House of the Moon.* New York: Warner Books, Inc., 1995.

Fitch, Ed. *Magical Rites From The Crystal Well.* St. Paul, Minn.: Llewellyn Publications, 1989.

Kerenyi, Karl. *Goddesses of Sun and Moon*. Translated from German by Murray Stein. Dallas: Spring Publications, Inc., 1979.

Kunz, George Frederick. *The Curious Lore of Precious Stones*. Copyright 1913 by J. B. Lippincott Company, Philadelphia, Pa.; copyright renewed 1941 by Ruby Kunz Zinsser; published 1971 by Dover Publications, Inc., New York, by special arrangement with J. P. Lippincott Company.

Malbrough, Ray T. *Charms, Spells & Formulas*. St. Paul, Minn.: Llewellyn Publications, 1986.

Medici, Marina. *Good Magic*. London: Mcmillan London Limited, London, England, 1988; New York: Prentice Hall Press, 1989.

Melody. *Love is in the Earth: A Kaleidoscope of Crystals*. Wheat Ridge, Colo.: Earth-Love Publishing House, 1995.

Monaghan, Patricia. *The Goddess Path*. St. Paul, Minn.: Llewellyn Publications, 1999.

———. *The New Book of Goddesses and Heroines*. St. Paul, Minn.: Llewellyn Publications, 1997.

Morrison, Dorothy. *Bud, Blossom & Leaf*. St. Paul, Minn.: Llewellyn Publications, 2001.

———. *Everyday Magic: Spells and Rituals for Modern Living*. St. Paul, Minn.: Llewellyn Publications, 1998.

———. *The Craft: A Witch's Book of Shadows*. St. Paul, Minn.: Llewellyn Publications, 2001.

Pharr, Daniel. *Moon Wise*. St. Paul, Minn.: Llewellyn Publications, 2000.

Riva, Anna. *The Modern Herbal Spellbook: The Magical Uses of Herbs*. Toluca Lake, Calif.: International Imports, 1974.

Slater, Herman. *The Magickal Formulary*. Copyright 1981 by Magickal Childe Inc., New York.

Stone, Merlin. *Ancient Mirrors of Womanhood*. Boston, Mass.: Beacon Press, 1979.

Telesco, Patricia. *Magick Made Easy*. New York: HarperSanFrancisco, 1999.

———. *Spinning Spells, Weaving Wonders*. Freedom, Calif.: Crossing Press, 1996.

Index